ORIGINS OF A PSYCHOPATH

ORIGINS OF A PSYCHOPATH

V. BRYAN

V Ly Publishing
Nephilim Imprint Books
1046 Church Rd, W 106-224
Southaven, MS 38671
www.endtimenephilim.com

ISBN: 978-0988681422

Dedication

To those who will read and come to know
the truth that will set them free.

Notes to the Reader

For simplicity, since the subject of this book was diagnosed as a psychopath, I will use that term, but know the source of both psychopaths and sociopaths has one and the same origin. I am not a psychologist or psychiatrist nor do I claim to be. However, with the help of these fields of study, along with the Bible, I invite the reader to take the path back to the origins of these evil ones in Origins of a Psychopath.

In order to provide the reader a backward march in time to discovery, one must deal with specific areas of behavior that repeat from one generation to the next. It is not my intent to offend anyone. For the purpose of this book, I will identify sin and iniquity according to Biblical standards to illuminate the cycles of destruction set against mankind.

Table of Contents

Foreword

My Wife the Author

I recently celebrated my 26th wedding anniversary with my wife Vickie, the author of *Origins of a Psychopath*. As I think about our life together, the best word to describe her is faithful. I am amazed when I think back over these years and realize that she doesn't falter in her faithfulness to God, to her family, and to her calling. She is sold out 100%. That is a very rare thing in this world. Before we met, I quoted these verses from Proverbs 31 in my prayers many times:

> 10An excellent wife, who can find? For her worth is far above jewels.11The heart of her husband trusts in her, And he will have no lack of gain.12She does him good and not evil All the days of her life. Proverbs 31:10-12 NASB

I would like the readers to know that the author of this book has been faithful to God, faithful to me and our children, and faithful in her preparation for Nephilim Imprint Books. She has spent several years studying 8-10 hours per day, six and sometimes seven days a week, in order to bring these books to you. Her dedication and faithfulness have culminated in the book in this reader's hand, as well as, the entire series on the Kingdoms of light and darkness. James Bryan

Introduction

As I sat across the table, I stared at one who sought to shatter our very existence. No remorse, no shame. Nothing mattered, but to protect the scheme of destruction set against us. Exposure of hidden lies was met by buckets of tears and even more lies. I locked onto her every move and then abruptly, a total transformation came over her. She just put on her mask. No more tears, not one. She went on her way as if our discussion never took place. I did not understand then, but I do now, and it is time to expose these deceivers in our midst.

Chapter 1

Masked People

Living among us are people that look like any other humans but are far from normal. They commit callous acts both cruel and inhumane. Understanding these people cannot be left to science alone. Recognizing their spiritual origins is a must. Whether called antisocial personality disorder, sociopaths, or psychopaths, they easily bring hell to those in their grasp. With these terms used interchangeably at times, consider some insight from segments of an article written by leaders in the field of psychopathy from an article "reprinted by permission from the FBI Law Enforcement Bulletin."

Over the years, Hollywood has provided many examples of psychopaths. As a result, psychopaths often are identified as scary people who look frightening or have other off-putting characteristics. In reality, a psychopath can be anyone—a neighbor, coworker, or homeless person. Each of these seemingly harmless people may prey continually on others around them.

Psychopathy and Personality Disorder

The term *psychopathy* refers to a personality disorder that includes a cluster of interpersonal, affective, lifestyle, and antisocial traits and behaviors.[1] These involve deception; manipulation; irresponsibility; impulsivity; stimulation seeking; poor behavioral controls; shallow affect; lack of empathy, guilt, or remorse; sexual promiscuity; callous disregard for the rights of others; and unethical and antisocial behaviors.[2] Psychopathy is the most dangerous of the personality disorders. To understand it, one must know some fundamental principles about personality.

Individuals' personalities represent who they are; they result from genetics and upbringing and reflect how persons view the world and think the world views them. Personalities dictate how people interact with others and how they cope with problems, both real and imagined. Individuals' personalities develop and evolve until approximately their late 20s, after which they are well-hardwired in place, unable to be altered.

Traits and Characteristics

Psychopathy is apparent in a specific cluster of traits and characteristics. These traits, ultimately, define adult psychopathy and begin to manifest themselves in early childhood.[3] The lifelong expression of this disorder is a product of complex interactions between biological and temperamental predispositions and social forces—in other words, the ways in which nature and nurture shape and define each other.[4]

Many psychopaths exhibit a profound lack of remorse for their aggressive actions, both violent and nonviolent, along with a corresponding lack of empathy for their victims. This central psychopathic concept enables them to act in a cold-blooded manner, using those around them as pawns to achieve goals and satisfy needs and desires, whether sexual, financial, physical, or emotional. Most psychopaths are grandiose, selfish sensation seekers who lack a moral compass—a conscience—and go through life taking what they want. They do not accept responsibility for their actions and find a way to shift the blame to someone or something else.

Chameleons and Predators

In general, psychopaths are glib and charming, and they use these attributes to manipulate others into trusting and believing in them. This may lead to people giving them money, voting them into office, or, possibly, being murdered by them. Because of their interpersonal prowess, most psychopaths can present themselves favorably on a first impression, and many function successfully in society.

Many of the attitudes and behaviors of psychopaths have a distinct predatory quality to them. Psychopaths see others as either competitive predators or prey. To understand how psychopaths achieve their goals, it is important to see them as classic predators. For instance, they surf the Internet looking for attractive persons to con or, even, murder and target retirees to charm them out of their life savings for a high-risk investment scam, later blaming them for being too trusting. Most psychopaths are skilled at camouflage through deception and manipulation, as well as stalking and locating areas where there is an endless supply of victims.[5] The psychopath is an interspecies predator, and peoples' visceral reaction to them—"they made the hair stand up on my neck"—is an early warning system driven by fear of being prey to a predator.[6]

The psychopath's egocentricity and need for power and control are the perfect ingredients for a lifetime of antisocial and criminal activity. The ease with which a psychopath can engage in violence holds significance for society and law enforcement. Often, psychopaths are shameless in their actions against others, whether it is murdering someone in a calculated, cold-blooded manner, manipulating law enforcement during an interview, or claiming remorse for actions, but blaming the victim for the crime. This particularly proves true in cases involving sexual offenders who are psychopathic.

If psychopaths commit a homicide, their killing likely will be planned and purposeful, not the result of a loss of emotional control; their motive more commonly will involve sadistic gratification.[7] When faced with overwhelming evidence of their guilt, they frequently will claim they lost control or were in a rage when committing the act of violence. In fact, their violence often is emotionless, calculated, and completely controlled.[8] If psychopaths commit a serious crime with another individual (almost always a non-psychopath), they often will avoid culpability by using the other individual to take the blame for the offense. Evidence suggests that this particular strategy is even more evident in serious multiple-perpetrator offences committed by a psychopathic youth with a non-psychopathic partner.[9]

Myth Busting

Many misconceptions about psychopaths can lead to mistakes in investigations, interviews, and court proceedings. Psychopaths are both male and female, but more men are psychopaths than women. They represent all races, cultures, and socioeconomic backgrounds. Some are intelligent, while others possess average or below-average intelligence. They come from both single- and two-parent households and may themselves be married with children.

Psychopaths understand right from wrong. They know they are subject to society's rules, but willingly disregard them to pursue their own interests. They also are not out of touch with reality. They rarely become psychotic unless they also have a separate mental illness or use powerful drugs, such as stimulants. These hallmarks of genuine mental illness might be proposed during a criminal defense, but they often are successfully challenged at trial.

Presence In Society

Many psychopaths have little difficulty joining the ranks of business, politics, law enforcement, government, and academia.[10] They exist in all lines of work, from executive to blue-collar professions. However, psychopathy often is misread, misdiagnosed, minimized, or explained away by professionals whose jobs require regular interaction with psychopaths, namely in the mental health, judicial, and law enforcement communities. When these professionals encounter psychopathy in the course of their work, their reaction and response to the psychopath may be too little and too late. Their lack of information can lead to believing a psychopath's complete fabrications as seemingly plausible.

Psychopaths differ from each other, and their condition can vary in severity. Current research suggests a continuum of psychopathy ranging from those who are highly psychopathic to persons who have the same number or fewer traits in a milder form. A clinical assessment of psychopathy is based on the person having the full cluster of psychopathic traits—at least to some degree—based on a pattern of lifetime behaviors.

Many psychopaths are not violent. However, those who display violence and sexual deviance are generally more dangerous than other offenders, and their likelihood of reoffending may be significantly higher.[12] Psychopaths tend to have longer, more varied, and more serious criminal histories and, overall, are more consistently violent than nonpsychopaths. Their use of violence appears to be less situational and more directed toward particular goals than the type of violence displayed by nonpsychopaths.[13] It is estimated that approximately 1 percent of the general male population are psychopaths, and 15 to 20 percent of the prison population are psychopathic.[14]

Given the risk that psychopathic offenders pose for society, their ability to potentially manipulate the authorities poses concern. Psychopathic killers more likely will deny charges brought against them, and some indication exists that they are able to manipulate the criminal justice system to receive reduced sentences and appeal sentences to a higher court.[15] Their acting ability can enable them to frequently manipulate and persuade members of a parole board to release them approximately 2.5 times faster than other offenders up for parole, despite their longer list of offenses and elevated risk.[17] Psychopaths can be adept at imitating emotions that they believe will mitigate their punishment.[18]

Research suggests that the linguistic patterns of psychopaths are unique compared with the patterns of non-psychopaths. Their stylistic differences reflect how they view the world around them, as well as their profound emotional deficit and detachment from emotional events.[19] However, psychopaths' lack of feeling and bonding to others allows them to have clarity in observing the behavior of their prey. They do not get caught in or bogged down by the anxieties and emotions that other people experience in social situations.

Victims

The reactions of psychopaths to the damage they inflict most likely will be cool indifference and a sense of power, pleasure, or smug satisfaction, rather than regret or concern. Most people closely associated with a psychopath may know something is wrong with that person, but have no idea as to the depth of the pathology. They frequently will blame themselves for all of the problems they have had with a psychopath, whether at work, in a relationship, or within a family. After interacting with psychopaths, most people are stunned by these individuals' ruthlessness, callousness, and denial or minimization of the damage they have caused.[1]

Chapter 2

Components of Psychopathy

"A study on twins by Dr. Essi Viding of the London Kings College Institute of Psychiatry found the tendency toward psychopathic behavior has a strong genetic component. The results of this study showed in children with psychopathic tendencies, antisocial behavior was strongly inherited. In contrast, the antisocial behavior of children who did not have psychopathic tendencies was mainly influenced by environmental factors. In antisocial 7-year-olds with callous and unemotional traits, Viding found, the antisocial behavior was strongly genetic in origin (a group heritability of 80%)."[2]

Another psychiatrist, Dr. Igor Galynker, M.D., Ph.D. of Beth Israel Medical Center New York, and NY, states:

"Psychopathy is biological and one of the most inherited human characteristics,"[3]

"These people really see you as a piece of furniture and the empathy that allows us to feel others' feelings is missing," he said. "These people are wired differently. Their brains are different."[4]

Along with the genetic and environmental factors involved in reproducing psychopaths, the "connections between the uncinate fasciculus (UF), which joins parts of the brain called the amygdala and the orbitofrontal cortex (OFC), differed significantly in psychopaths verses normal people. The brain function of the amygdala is involved in emotional responses such as fear, disgust and pleasure, while the OFC is involved in higher decision-making." [5] [6] [7] Such abnormality confirms that psychopaths are not as other humans. Factors such as brain injuries, genetics, environment, socialization, and nurturing are all aspects of psychopathy, but an essential key is found in spiritual laws.

Chapter 3

Establish the Path

I must lay a foundation of truth by the Bible to journey back in time to expose the *Origins of a Psychopath*. I will attempt brevity as these points are covered in greater depth in my book, *Living with the Nephilim, the Seed of Destruction*. These principles must be established for all who read. First and foremost I am exposing the enemy which comes from the spiritual realm and greatly affects life on earth. One can tell what is going on in the supernatural by what is going on in the world and the affairs of mankind.

In the Bible, the Book of Genesis describes how the events of creation came out of the spirit realm into the natural world by God's spoken word and the work of the Holy Spirit. The heavens, earth, and all therein, along with the first man, his wife, and the generations, came forth as described in Genesis chapters 1-5. Two spiritual kingdoms are in our midst: the Kingdom of God and the

Kingdom of Satan, which are eternal and unseen by our eyes.

Satan, once a holy angel, chose to rebel against God and completely transformed to evil, as is the kingdom he rules. Satan lured one third of all angels to join his apostasy and attempted a coup in heaven. They were overpowered and thrown out. On earth in the Garden of Eden, Satan went to work and enticed Adam and Eve to sin. Once Adam and Eve broke their covenant with God, Satan gained access to their lives. Spiritual and physical death came to them and to all mankind, cutting them off from a Holy God. Adam had been given charge over earth but lost it when the devil successfully stole his God-given position of authority. Satan then became the ruler over the world in which we live. Satan does not own the earth but obtained the right to rule man's world.

Adam's authority was lost by his disobedience to a command from God. An all-important principal needs to be understood: submit to the Kingdom of God and reap the benefits from the kingdom. Rebellion against the Kingdom of God gives opportunity for satanic attack and loss of those benefits. Satan's rebellion made him a law breaker and the leader of the lawless ones. God is holy and light; nothing in him is darkness. By contrast

Satan instills darkness in behavior and thoughts to attempt to keep the understanding of the light of God's Word from shining on the heart of man. Otherwise, just because of the wonder and the absolute awesomeness of creation itself, humans would understand everything came about by the designs of one greater than us.

> This is the message we have heard from Him and announce to you, that God is Light, and in Him there is no darkness at all.
> 1 John 1:5 NASB

Chapter 4

God's Order for Mankind

God's precedence for human life was set by him in the beginning of man's life on earth, and God gave man commands to follow in order to reap the benefit of His blessings. Each individual human was created to be spiritually united to God. God displayed this by creation of Adam alone before God provided him a wife. Covenantal agreements between God and men made it clear what God required and were similar to a contract in which parties involved agree to specific requirements as stated in the contract. As long as the parties submit to the stipulations, they reap the contracts benefits. If they break the contract, then loss of the benefits and consequences arise. A covenantal relationship existed between God and Adam in which God provided all he would need for life on earth. Adam's part was to honor Him as God alone and walk in obedience to His commands and ordinances. As long as Adam did this, the blessing from God remained. Before God gave Adam his second covenantal relationship, he was well established in his first with God himself. Then God prepared a wife for Adam and brought her to him. Marriage became the foundational covenant for a family. By forsaking all others, a husband and wife joined as one, with their children born and reared in the sanctification of their marriage covenant with benefit of both parents.

> Has not [the LORD] made them one? In flesh and spirit they are his. And why one? Because he was seeking godly offspring. So guard yourself in your spirit, and do not break faith with the wife of your youth. Malachi 2:15 NIV

Not everybody is called to be married. The apostle Paul viewed his lack of marriage as a gift in order to be devoted to God. So where ever the reader may be in terms of family relationship, may God's will take place.

As the one who usurped control of man's world, Satan took aim to destroy every covenant instituted by God. Satan's means to do so would involve corruption of God's order for human life. When people accept that which opposes God's Word, it sets them in rebellion to God's kingdom. Satan knows God's Word will be violated. When God's Word is violated, God's righteousness rises up to oppose the violation and without repentance, God's judgment falls (Romans 2:5) Satan lures people into sin, so he may bring about their destruction as scripture tells us, "Satan comes to kill, steal and destroy" (James 1:13-15, John 10:10).

> We know that we are of God, and that the whole world lies in the power of the evil one.1 John 5:19 NASB

Chapter 5

Fathers - An Accounting System

The Lord is slow to anger and abundant in loving kindness, forgiving iniquity and transgression; but He will by no means clear the guilty, visiting the iniquity of the fathers on the children to the third and the fourth generations.' Numbers 14:18 NASB

A sin is a "transgression of God's known will or any principle or law regarded as embodying this."[8] Sin transfers from one generation to the next through the iniquity of the fathers onto their children to the third and fourth generations (Exodus 20:5, 7, Duet. 5:9-10).[9] Another term for this is generational sin, because a particular sin or transgression can be found from generation to generation in a family line. Some might think, "Wait a minute. What about mothers?" We see transferable sin from mothers, but a father is accountable to God as the head of his family. From the beginning God has kept up with mankind by fathers as Biblical genealogies are listed by a father and their male offspring. One can read this in Numbers 26:2 when Moses took a census of Israel and also divided land, both by their father's.[2]

> Take a census of all the males of the congregation of the Israelites by families, by their fathers' houses, according to the number of names, head by head. Numbers 26:2 Amplified Bible

> "But the land shall be divided by lot. They shall receive their inheritance according to the names of the tribes of their fathers. Numbers 26:55 NASB

At times females are mentioned in a Biblical genealogy, but for the most part we do not know mothers or daughters (Matthew 1:5, Numbers 26:33). A man's body produces male and female seed which determines gender, and both sexes are the recipients of their father's transference of iniquity. [10] We see this truth in the beginning of creation.

In Genesis 1:27, "God created man he **him;** **male and female,** created "he" "them." This scripture tells us **"him" was male and female.** The King James Bible brings this point out with living creatures.

> 21And God created great whales, and every living creature that moveth, which the waters brought forth abundantly, after their kind, and every winged fowl **after his kind:** and God saw that it was good Genesis 1:21 KJV

> 24And God said, Let the earth bring forth the living creature **after his kind,** cattle, and creeping thing, and beast of the earth **after his kind:** and it was so. 25And God made the beast of the earth after **his** kind, and cattle after their kind, and every- thing that creepeth upon the earth **after his kind:** and God saw that *it was* good. Genesis 1:24-25 KJV

Living creatures were made after **his** kind, and once God created a male, He followed with **his** female of like kind. A male set the pattern for his female, and in turn, he set the pattern for his offspring. Genesis chapter five states the same truth for humans. A male and female were called he and he was a them, and both were called Adam. Both male and female were blessed to prosper by their Creator.[11]

> Male and female created **he them;** and blessed them, and called their name Adam, in the day when they were created. Genesis 5:2 KJV

By this design of our Creator, a lineage of a male's family line can be traced back to the previous generations clearly through fathers, whose surname and Y chromosome pass to their sons as explained in this paragraph from the *Human Genome Project*. It seems God keeps track of humans through their fathers, but did not leave mothers out by mitochondrial DNA (mtDNA).

> "When DNA is passed from one generation to the next, most of it is mixed by the processes that make each person unique from his or her parents. Some special pieces of DNA, however, remain virtually unaltered as they pass from parent to child. One of these pieces is carried by the Y chromosome, which is passed only from father to son. Another

piece, mitochondrial DNA (mtDNA), is passed (with few exceptions) only from mother to child. Since the DNA in the Y chromosome does not mix with other DNA, it is like a genetic surname that allows men to trace their paternal lineages. Similarly, mtDNA allows both men and women to trace their maternal lineages." [12]

In Numbers 14:18, "visiting the iniquity of the fathers on the children to the third and the fourth generations," the word for "children" is *ben* in Hebrew. *Ben* means "a son or grandson as the builder of a family line and also can mean, children, both male and female." [13] Since "children" in this scripture was translated from *ben,* one again sees God's organization of family lines through fathers. The male is the builder of his family line, and iniquity transfers from him to his children, both male and female, then to the next generations.

You show unfailing love to thousands, but you also bring the consequences of one generation's sin upon the next. You are the great and powerful God, the LORD of Heaven's Armies. Jeremiah 32:18 NLT

God does not treat those who love him as their sins deserve, but sin still brings consequences (Psalms 103:10, Psalm 78:38). What is iniquity? Iniquity defined, "a violation of right or duty; wicked act; sin."[14] In Numbers 14:18, *avon*, the Hebrew word for iniquity means, "perversity, depravity, guilt or, consequence of or punishment for iniquity." [15]

> The Lord is slow to anger and abundant in loving kindness, forgiving iniquity and transgression; but He will by no means clear the guilty, visiting the iniquity of the fathers on the children to the third and the fourth generations. Numbers 14:18 NASB

Look again at Numbers 14:18 and the phrase "visiting the iniquity." Visit means "to go to," so iniquity of a father visits, or goes to, every one of his children, grand and great grandchildren. The visit seeks to transfer the sin of a father onto the next generations. This may extend beyond the third and fourth generation if a father engages the iniquity and passes it on to repeat the process.[16] Recall mothers are not excluded, but one must look to her father to see the iniquity flow which moves through both sexes to affect the generations.

A natural way iniquity repeats from one generation to the next comes by contact with our families. In our day, two to three generations, and possibly more, of a family line may be alive at once. With family members are around one another, they become accustomed to each other's way of life. Such closeness in families makes it easy for members to observe behaviors, either right or wrong, and copy them. This similarly occurs with anyone else one spends time with, along with any activities. One can see how sins and iniquities may easily pass through these generations. What about a child who does not know his or her biological family? It does not matter. This is a spiritual law and iniquity of the fathers will still visit that child. God set spiritual precedence for mankind by His Word, and any violation authorizes iniquity to pass on to the generations. Satan keeps iniquity moving with instigation coming from the spirit realm.

From one generation to the next, a transition of how iniquity plays out may occur; this depends on individuals and the choices they make. If a man steals, then that visits his children, grandchildren, and great grandchildren, and each one may become a thief or some other kind of criminal. Additionally, the sin opens the door for anyone in this family line to be victimized by such activity due to iniquity passed on from ancestors.

A Biblical example of iniquity and the different ways it played out in a family line can be observed in the life of King David, which began by the sexual sin of adultery.

> But the thing that David had done was evil in the sight of the LORD. 2 Samuel 11:27b NASB

He took another man's wife for sex and arranged her husband's death to hide his adultery. Once the woman's husband was killed, King David married the man's wife.

> 9 'Why have you despised the word of the LORD by doing evil in His sight? You have struck down Uriah the Hittite with the sword, have taken his wife to be your wife, and have killed him with the sword of the sons of Ammon. 10'Now therefore, the sword shall never depart from your house, because you have despised Me and have taken the wife of Uriah the Hittite to be your wife.' 11"Thus says the LORD, 'Behold, I will raise up evil against you from your own household; I will even take your wives before your eyes and give them to your companion, and he

will lie with your wives in broad daylight. 12'Indeed you did it secretly, but I will do this thing before all Israel and under the sun.'" 13Then David said to Nathan, "I have sinned against the LORD." And Nathan said to David, "The LORD also has taken away your sin; you shall not die. 14"However, because by this deed you have given occasion to the enemies of the LORD to blaspheme, the child also that is born to you shall surely die."
2 Samuel 12:9-14 NASB

An important key for King David was that once confronted with his sin, King David repented. After King David's death, God referred to him as "My servant David whom I chose, who observed My commandments and My statutes (1 Kings 11:34)." But this did not stop iniquity that gained access to his family line (2 Samuel 12:13). Consequences of his sins were declared to King David by Nathan, a prophet of God, and it was not good. "The sword would never leave his house, evil would rise up against King David from his household, his wives would be taken and one close would have sex with them in broad daylight, and the son conceived in the act of adultery would die" (2 Samuel 12:9-14).

How did iniquity actually play out in King David's family line? His children's lives tell the story. King David's sin with Bathsheba began as a sexual transgression, so sexual transgressions found a way into the next generation. Tamar, one of King David's virgin daughters, was raped by her half-brother.

> 11But as she was feeding him, he grabbed her and demanded, "Come to bed with me, my darling sister."12"No, my brother!" she cried. "Don't be foolish! Don't do this to me! Such wicked things aren't done in Israel. 13Where could I go in my shame? And you would be called one of the greatest fools in Israel. Please, just speak to the king about it, and he will let you marry me." 14But Amnon wouldn't listen to her, and since he was stronger than she was, he raped her. 1 Samuel 13:11-14 NLT

Tamar begged Amnon to stop his assault; she did not want such shame upon her (2 Samuel 13). Tamar had done nothing wrong, but iniquity seized Amnon to move through and stuck King David's next generation. Amnon victimized and then despised his sister, which forever changed her life.

15Then suddenly Amnon's love turned to hate, and he hated her even more than he had loved her. "Get out of here!" he snarled at her.16"No, no!" Tamar cried. "Sending me away now is worse than what you've already done to me." But Amnon wouldn't listen to her. 17He shouted for his servant and demanded, "Throw this woman out, and lock the door behind her!" 18So the servant put her out and locked the door behind her. She was wearing a long, beautiful robe, as was the custom in those days for the king's virgin daughters. 19But now Tamar tore her robe and put ashes on her head. And then, with her face in her hands, she went away crying.20Her brother Absalom saw her and asked, "Is it true that Amnon has been with you? Well, my sister, keep quiet for now, since he's your brother. Don't you worry about it?" So Tamar lived as a desolate woman in her brother Absalom's house. 21When King David heard what had happened, he was very angry. 22And though Absalom never spoke to Amnon about this, he hated Amnon deeply because of what he had done to his sister.2 Samuel 13:15-22 NLT

The second phase of King David's sin with Bathsheba involved murder, with the arranged death of Bathsheba's husband. Similarly, Tamar's brother Absalom, another son of King David, plotted to have Amnon killed in revenge for the rape of his sister Tamar (2 Samuel 13:32).

23Two years later, when Absalom's sheep were being sheared at Baal-hazor near Ephraim, Absalom invited all the king's sons to come to a feast. 24He went to the king and said, "My sheep-shearers are now at work. Would the king and his servants please come to celebrate the occasion with me?" 25The king replied, "No, my son. If we all came, we would be too much of a burden on you." Absalom pressed him, but the king would not come, though he gave Absalom his blessing. 26"Well, then," Absalom said, "if you can't come, how about sending my brother Amnon with us?" "Why Amnon?" the king asked. 27But Absalom kept on pressing the king until he finally agreed to let all his sons attend, including Amnon. So Absalom prepared a feast fit for a king. 28Absalom told his men, "Wait until Amnon gets drunk; then at my signal, kill him! Don't be afraid. I'm the one who has given the command. Take courage and do it!" 29So at Absalom's signal they murdered Amnon. 2 Samuel 13:23-28 NLTIt was also Absolom who committed adultery with his father's concubines as Nathan the prophet declared. A tent was pitched so all Israel would know, which brought public shame to King David in broad daylight. King David tried to hide his sins, so adultery committed against him was openly displayed. His own children were evildoers against his house (I Samuel 16:21-22). This generation after King David made iniquities' path quite easy. All this occurred because of the spiritual law stated in Numbers 14:18. We have not mentioned King Solomon here, but iniquity from his father definitely worked against him as well.

Now to comprehend how iniquity gained access to Amnon, let's back up to find out what happened.

1Now David's son Absalom had a beautiful sister named Tamar.

And Amnon, her half-brother, fell desperately in love with her. 2 Amnon became so obsessed with Tamar that he became ill. She was a virgin, and Amnon thought he could never have her. 3But Amnon had a very crafty friend—his cousin Jonadab. He was the son of David's brother Shimea. 4One day Jonadab said to Amnon, "What's the trouble? Why should the son of a king look so dejected morning after morning?" So Amnon told him, "I am in love with Tamar, my brother Absalom's sister." 5"Well," Jonadab said, "I'll tell you what to do. Go back to bed and pretend you are ill. When your father comes to see you, ask him to let Tamar come and prepare some food for you. Tell him you'll feel better if she prepares it as you watch and feeds you with her own hands." 2 Samuel 13:1-5 NLT

Verse 2 is a key: Amnon became obsessed with having sex with Tamar to the point of illness. Temptation arose from his own lust which Amnon did not control and allowed to get stronger. Maybe he replayed over and over in his mind what it would be like to have sex with her. Then finally, he shared his lustful desire with a "crafty friend" who happened to be his cousin. Crafty means "Skillful in underhand or evil schemes; cunning; deceitful; sly," which indicated evil influence from a person who gave Amnon wicked advice. The word "crafty" described Satan in the Garden of Eden before the fall of Adam and Eve. Satan, an evil spirit, enticed Adam and Eve to sin via the serpent. So crafty advice was just what the devil ordered to gain access to King David's offspring. This advice made the way for iniquity to be passed on to them.[17]

> Now the serpent was more crafty than any beast of the field which the LORD God had made. And he said to the woman, "Indeed, has God said, 'You shall not eat from *any tree of the garden'?"
> Genesis 3:15 NASB

Iniquity's ploy to seize Absalom as a vessel likewise came by way of foolish advice. This advice came at a time when Absalom sought to take the throne from his father. King David prayed that Ahithophel's advice to Absalom would be foolishness, but interestingly, it was that foolish advice that persuaded Absalom's public display of sexual immorality with his father's concubines (2 Samuel 15:31).

> 20Then Absalom turned to Ahithophel and asked him, "What should I do next?" 21Ahithophel told him, "Go and

sleep with your father's concubines, for he has left them here to look after the palace. Then all Israel will know that you have insulted your father beyond hope of reconciliation, and they will throw their support to you." 22So they set up a tent on the palace roof where everyone could see it, and Absalom went in and had sex with his father's concubines.23Absalom followed Ahithophel's advice, just as David had done. For every word Ahithophel spoke seemed as wise as though it had come directly from the mouth of God. 2 Samuel 16:20-23 NLT

Iniquities mandate visits upon the children to repeat the sins of their father's. Both Amnon and Absalom transgressed into sexual sin, and both were killed, a reflection of King David's sin and iniquities

8For the battle there was spread over the whole countryside, and the forest devoured more people that day than the sword devoured. 9Now Absalom happened to meet the servants of

David. For Absalom was riding on [his] mule, and the mule went under the thick branches of a great oak. And his head caught fast in the oak, so he was left hanging between heaven and earth, while the mule that was under him kept going. 10When a certain man saw [it], he told Joab and said, "Behold, I saw Absalom hanging in an oak." 11Then Joab said to the man who had told him, "Now behold, you saw [him]! Why then did you not strike him there to the ground? And I would have given you ten [pieces] of silver and a belt." 12The man said to Joab, "Even if I should receive a thousand [pieces of] silver in my hand, I would not put out my hand against the king's son; for in our hearing the king charged you and Abishaiand Ittai, saying, Protect for me the young man Absalom!' 13"Otherwise, if I had dealt treacherously against his life (and there is nothing hidden from the king), then you yourself would have stood aloof." 14Then Joab said, "I will not waste time here with you." So he took three spears in his hand and thrust them through the heart of

Absalom while he was yet alive in the midst of the oak. 15And ten young men who carried Joab's armor gathered around and struck Absalom and killed him. 2 Samuel 18:8-15 NASB

Chapter 6

Sin Opens the Door

From one generation to the next, sin opens and keeps doors open for iniquity to repeat. God's Word and its importance must be taken into account to understand the origins of psychopaths for the problem is spiritual and physical (Isaiah 55:11).

> So will My word be which goes forth from My mouth; *It will not* return to Me empty, Without accomplishing what I desire, And without succeeding in the matter for which I sent it. Isaiah 55:11 NASB

Sin comes through lustful desire arising from a person's own fallen, sin nature, and each person has his or her own forte for sin. Even so, iniquity comes along from prior generations to seek a path as well.

13Let no one say when he is tempted, "I am being tempted by God"; for God cannot be tempted by evil, and He Himself does not tempt anyone. 14But each one is tempted when he is carried away and enticed by his own lust. 15Then when lust has conceived, it gives birth to sin; and when sin is accomplished, it brings forth death. James 1:13-15 ESV

Iniquity finds its pathway through enticement by evil spirits called devils and demons. These spirits work alongside family lines to initiate repetition of sin in the next generations. An evil spirit may be identified by the condition it brings or the result of its presence according to the example Jesus gave us (Luke 8:30, Luke 11:14). In Luke 8:30 Jesus asked the ruling spirit within a man his name. A name identifies a particular person, and by his or her name a person is recognized.

And Jesus asked him, "What is your name?" And he said, "Legion"; for many demons had entered him. Luke 8:30 NASB

> And He was casting out a demon, and it was mute; when the demon had gone out, the mute man spoke; and the crowds were amazed. Luke 11:14 NASB

With this in mind consider the first family and another Biblical example of iniquity that moved from Adam to Cain. The spirit of death acquired access to Adam's lineage by his disobedience to God's Word. Temptation to sin approached Adam's son Cain, who yielded to the urges, and a devil acquired access to him. Thus an evil spirit gained an open door to move through Cain.

> 6 Then the LORD said to Cain, "Why are you angry? And why has your countenance fallen? 7 "If you do well, will not *your countenance* be lifted up? And if you do not do well, **sin is crouching at the door;** and its desire is for you, but you must master it." Genesis 4:6-7 NASB

The spirit of death acquired access to Abel through Cain. Death changed its form in this generation. Abel's death became the first murder on earth. Satan gained access to not only Cain, but to his descendants as well (Genesis 4:1-8). As a consequence of sin, Cain became a nomadic, wanderer who reaped a cursed ground that no longer produced as before (Genesis 4:14). Cain took Abel's life, so Cain lost the life he previously enjoyed about his family. Cain left the Presence of God, which was separation from God, and went to the land of Nod (wandering) where his first son Enoch was born.[18] Cain then built a walled city for protection, an indication that Cain still feared someone would murder him, just as he did his brother (Genesis 4:11-16).

> 17 Cain had relations with his wife and she conceived, and gave birth to Enoch; and he built a city, and called the name of the city Enoch, after the name of his son. 18 Now to Enoch was born Irad and Irad became the father of Mehujael, and Mehujael became the father of Methushael, and Methushael became the father of Lamech. Genesis 4:17-18 NASB

Not much information is given in Scripture about the descendants of Cain, but Hebrew names and their meanings give insight. By these one may recognize sin's transference through Cain's family line (Genesis 17:5).[19]

Enoch's name is defined as "dedicated," as this first city was dedicated to Cain's son. Enoch's son Irad's name means, "Fugitive or wild ass."

Mehujael means "smitten by God," and Methushael, "man of God, or suppliant." Irad, a fugitive, indicates lawlessness. Mehujael, Irad's son, was struck down by God, which conveys he also was an evil man. Son of Mehujael, Methushael's name indicates he became a "man of God." In any family line a person can reject sin and turn to God, as it seems Methushael may have done. Then consider Lamech from Cain's lineage that killed a man and a boy. Lamech furthermore became the first polygamist who took two wives.[20][21][22][23][24]

Iniquity visits to the third and fourth generation. We will begin with Cain and do not know much about Cain's son, Enoch. But his grandson Irad was named as a fugitive. Next, his son in the fourth generation, Mehujael, was so evil God put an end to him. In the fifth generation Methushael cried out to God. Lamech, Methushael son, commits murders and marries two women at once. Lamech was the third generation from Irad, the fugitive. Each father may have his sins repeat to the third and fourth generations, as occurred from Irad. In Cain's family line, we note lawlessness, murder, fugitives, and one so evil God struck him down. Also, from Cain's line the marriage covenant established by God became altered.

After Cain murdered Abel, God enabled Adam and Eve to conceive another son, Seth. Let's take a look at his lineage.

---

6 Seth lived one hundred and five years, and became the father of Enosh. 9 Enosh lived ninety years, and became the father of Kenan. 12 Kenan lived seventy years, and became the father of Mahalalel. 13 Then Kenan lived eight hundred and forty years after he became the father of Mahalalel ... and he had other sons and daughters. 15 Mahalalel lived sixty-five years, and became the father of Jared. 18 Jared lived one hundred and sixty-two years, and became the father of Enoch. 21 Enoch lived sixty-five years, and became the father of Methuselah. 23 So all the days of Enoch were three hundred and sixty-five years. 24 Enoch walked with God; and he was not, for God took him. 25 Methuselah lived one hundred and eighty-seven years, and became the father of Lamech. 28 Lamech lived one hundred and eighty-two years, and became the father of a son. 29 Now he called his name Noah, saying, "This one will give us rest from our work and from the toil of our hands arising from the ground which the LORD has cursed." 30 Then Lamech lived five hundred and

ninety-five years after he became the father of Noah, and he had other sons and daughters. 32 Noah was five hundred years old, and Noah became the father of Shem, Ham, and Japheth. Genesis 5:6,9,12,13,15,18,21,25,27,28-30 NASB

By definitions let's see what we can find. Seth's first son Enosh's name, means "man." Enosh's son Kenan's name means "possession." Kenan's son Mahalaleel's name means "praise of God." Mahalaleel's son Jared means, "Descent." Jared had a son named Enoch, whose name indicates life and "dedicated" to God. He pleased God so much God took him to heaven without dying (Genesis 5:24). Enoch's son Methuselah's name was "man of the dart," who lived longer than any other in the Bible and after his death, the flood came. Methuselah also had a son he named Lamech, who became the father of Noah. Lamech is defined as "powerful," and Noah's name means "rest." By Noah's faith and trust in God, he demonstrated the way to find "rest." Noah believed God's Word, which saved him and his family from destruction. [25 26 27 28 29 30 31]

Both Cain and Seth had the same parents but turned out so differently. Cain and Seth made drastically different choices for their lives. Cain did not resist evil, so evil overcame him, and then evil moved through his descendants. Seth chose righteousness, and his descendants walked in the blessing of his decision.

Ezekiel 28 gives an overview of how each person can decide whether he or she will follow in the ways of the previous generation.

4"Behold, all souls are Mine; the soul of the father as well as the soul of the son is Mine. The soul who sins will die. 5"But if a man is righteous and practices justice and righteousness, 6and does not eat at the mountain [shrines] or lift up his eyes to the idols of the house of Israel, or defile his neighbor's wife or approach a woman during her menstrual period-- 7if a man does not oppress anyone, but restores to the debtor his pledge, does not commit robbery, [but] gives his bread to the hungry and covers the naked with clothing, 8if he does not lend [money] on interest or take increase, [if] he keeps his hand from iniquity [and] executes true~ justice between man and man, 9[if] he walks in My statutes and My ordinances so as to deal faithfully-- he is righteous [and] will surely live," declares the Lord GOD. 10"Then he may have a violent son who sheds blood and who does any of these things to a brother 11(though he himself did not do any of these things), that is, he even eats at the mountain [shrines], and defiles his neighbor's wife, 12oppresses the poor and needy, commits robbery, does not restore a pledge, but lifts up his eyes to the idols [and] commits abomination, 13he lends [money] on interest and takes increase; will he live? He will not live! He has committed all these abominations, he will surely be put to death; his blood will be on his own head. 14"Now behold, he has a son who has observed all his father's sins which he committed, and observing does not do likewise. 15"He does not eat at the mountain [shrines] or lift up his eyes to the idols of the house of Israel, or defile his neighbor's wife, 16or oppress anyone, or retain a pledge, or commit robbery, [but] he gives his bread to the hungry and covers the naked with clothing, 17he keeps his hand from the poor, does not take interest or increase, [but] executes My ordinances, and walks in My statutes; he will not die for his father's iniquity, he will surely live. 18"As for his father, because he practiced extortion, robbed [his] brother and did what was not good among his people, behold, he will die for his iniquity. Ezekiel 28:4-18 NASB

Chapter 7

Learn from Adolf Hitler

To take this study past Biblical times, a well-known, psychopath was needed, and the first one that came to my mind was Adolf Hitler. When researching Adolf Hitler, I found many differences in opinions on available information. By using the principal of Numbers 14:18, along with his family and personal life, consider patterns of iniquity passed down to the third and fourth generations in his family line. Then readers can take aspects of their lives and apply Biblical truths to understand what happened to create a murderer of millions.

Out of necessity during WWII, the United States needed to psychologically understand Adolf Hitler. Informants who knew Hitler provided information needed for the psychoanalysis as requested by the Office of Strategic Services (OSS). "In one of two similar reports, *A Psychological Profile of Adolf*

Hitler: His Life and Legend, was performed by psychoanalyst Walter C. Langer along with three other collaborators.[32] The second report entitled *Analysis of the Personality of Adolph Hitler* was performed by Dr. Henry A. Murray[33] All gathered material for the psychoanalysis consisted of over one thousand pages called the *Hitler Source Book."* [34] "Mr. Langer concluded if Germany neared defeat, suicide would be one of Adolf Hitler's options, which he did on April 30, 1945, with his wife of one day, Eva Braun."[35] Those involved in reviewing the gathered information came to the same opinion of Hitler's condition

"A general agreement among the collaborators determined that Hitler was probably a neurotic psychopath bordering on schizophrenia. This meant that he was not insane in the commonly accepted sense of the term, but a neurotic who lacked adequate inhibitions. It also meant there was a definite moral component in his character no matter how deeply it may have been distorted."[36]

The word "probably" was used due to source of the information instead of a doctor patient relationship. Here is a credible conclusion: Adolf Hitler was a "psychopath."[37] What a horrific diagnosis for those who did not understand the man in their midst.

"Adolf Hitler was born on April 20, 1889, in Braunau Am Inn, Austria, to Alois and Klara Hitler. [38] Adolf's father, Alois Schicklgruber, was the son of an unmarried, peasant woman named Maria Anna Schicklgruber. [39] She gave birth to Alois in 1837 when she was forty-two years old and refused to reveal the identity of his biological father. On his birth certificate 'illegitimate' was stamped instead of a father's name."[40, 41]

"There were three men most historians believe could have been his biological father. His mother married one of them, Johann Georg Hiedler, when Alois was five years old.[42] Upon Maria's death at the age of 52, Alois lived with his married step uncle, Johann Nepomuk Hiedler."[43] Nepomuk was also thought to be Alois's biological father, as he left Alois a portion of his inheritance. [44]

"At the time of her pregnancy Maria Schicklgruber was a servant on a farm owned by a Jewish family. [45] It has been speculated the heir of that farm, Leopold Frankenberger, at age nineteen conceived Alois with Maria.[46] Maria received financial support from the Frankenberger family of Graz, so this is feasible as well." [47] Mr. Langer included a fourth theory

"There are some people who seriously doubt that Johann Georg Hiedler was the father of Alois. Thyssen and Koehler, for example, claim that Chancellor Dollfuss had ordered the Austrian police to conduct a thorough investigation into the Hitler family. As a result of this investigation a secret document was prepared which proved that Maria Anna Schicklgruber was living in Vienna at the time she conceived. At that time she was employed as a servant in the home of Baron Rothschild. As soon as the family discovered her pregnancy she was sent back to her home in Spital where Alois was born. If it is true that one of the Rothschilds is the real father of Alois Hitler, it would make Adolph a quarter Jew. According to these sources, Adolph Hitler knew of the existence of this document and the incriminating evidence it contained. In order to obtain it he precipitated events in Austria and initiated the assassination of Dollfuss. According to this story, he failed to obtain the document at that time, since Dollfuss had secreted it and, had told Schuschnigg of its whereabouts so that in the event of his death the independence of Austria would remain assured."

Around forty years of age, Alois asserted
that the man who married his mother, Johann
Georg Hiedler, was his father and legally
changed his name. [49] "Thought to be a
clerical misspelling at the time of filing,
Alois' name officially became Hitler instead
of Hiedler."[50]

At some point, Alois developed a strong
sexual desire for women and a taste for
alcohol. Notorious for unfaithfulness and
numerous affairs, Alois married a total of
three times. At age thirty-six, he first married
a wealthy woman in poor health, thirteen
years older than he.[51] This marriage obviously
meant nothing to him, as he continued his
lifestyle of immorality and "moved a nineteen
year old, bar maid (Fannie Matzelsberger) in
with him, in a separate apartment from his
wife."[52] Johann Nepomuk Hiedler's had a
granddaughter named Klara Pölzl, and as
Alois' neice, she called him "Uncle." Nothing
unusual here, but when Klara became
orphaned, her Uncle Alois took her in with his
first wife as their foster daughter. With Alois´
sexual appetite, a sexual relationship with
Klara began at some point which points to
incest and maybe even pedophilia. Fannie did
not want Klara around as a "daughter," since
their ages were close. Klara was sent away.
[53]Think about this: Alois' niece became his
daughter and Fannie's competition while he
was still married to his first wife. His first wife
had enough and divorced Alois on the grounds
of adultery in 1880. [54] While married to his first
wife, just as his biological father had done,
Alois conceived a son with a woman not his

wife." The child, Alois Jr., retained his mother's name, Matzelsberger, at the time of his birth. At forty-five years of age, Alois married the twenty-one year old mother of Alois Jr. and gave the boy his last name. His second wife, Fannie Matzelsberger, gave birth to a daughter the next year, named Angela, and then Fannie soon fell ill."[55]

Upon Fannie's illness, Alois sent for Klara to care for his sick wife and their young children.[56] Then Fannie died in 1884. At some point during this time Alois and Klara conceived one or possibly two babies before they married in 1885. "William Patrick Hitler, nephew of Adolf Hitler, indicated an illegitimate child was born and died before Alois and Klara's marriage. Then the birth of a son came five to six months after they wed, who also died at a young age."[57]

In all, there were possibly eight children born to Klara and only two survived to adulthood.[58] On April 20, 1889, Klara gave birth to a frail Adolf Hitler when Alois was about fifty-two years old. [59] The family doctor, Dr. Bloch, recalls another daughter at their house described as an "imbecilic," but the family kept her hidden due to her condition. This daughter could be the child born and died before they married. Dr. Bloch believed a problem existed with the family blood since some of their children were retarded.

"With a common ancestor of Alois' grandfather and Karla's great-grandfather, incestuous blood existed as well. Then again, syphilis could also have been a factor"[60] So how many men marry their niece or daughter? Even though Karla was called Alois' foster daughter, what kind of a man does this? Keep on reading, as one goes back in history, this will be seen again. [61]

Career wise Alois did well and advanced to become a full inspector of customs in Austria. In 1895, Alois retired and moved his family to a farm. The next year Karla gave birth to another daughter named Paula. Paula was Adolf Hitler's only full biological sibling and considered as a person of low intelligence.[62] Paula's birth added a fifth child to the Hitler household.

Once Alois retired, his arrogance was remembered by his Austrian neighbors. Alois would wear his customs uniform to be formally addressed by his title. [63] Alois commonly strut himself about to look down on those around him. Alois failed at farming and moved his family again. With a twenty-three year difference between him and Klara, Alois spent a good bit of time away from his family. He liked to drink and socialize at local taverns and obviously left Klara with the children.[64]

"Called an absolute tyrant, William Patrick Hitler relayed accounts from his own father Alois Jr. that Alois would brutally beat his wife, children, and even their dog." [65] "Such beatings left Alois Jr. unconscious and Adolf was left as dead."[66] "A village mayor from Leonding admitted that Alois was 'awfully rough' with his wife and 'hardly ever spoke a word to her at home'." [67] Alois's violence and possible rape of Klara around their children made lasting harm to Adolf, as written by Mr. Langer. [68] As we find out about Alois, one wonders if his children truly died of disease or by his violent hands. Nothing seemed to hinder Alois Hitler from doing anything he wanted. In 1903 at age sixty-six, Alois Sr. died leaving Adolf and Paula with Klara. Four years later in 1907, Klara died of breast cancer. [69]

Adolf Hitler's self-written life story, *MEIN KAMPF,* told the German people what he wanted them to believe about his childhood.[70] Adolf Hitler gave a scenario of a perfect family life as a child. Mr. Langer's psychoanalysis provided a more accurate picture of what most likely occurred in Adolf's home as a child.[71]

"In MEIN KAMPF Hitler tries to create the impression that his home was rather peaceful and quiet, his "father a faithful civil servant, the mother devoting herself to the cares of the household and looking after her children with eternally the same loving care. It would seem that if this is a true representation of the home environment there would be no reason for his concealing it so scrupulously."[72]

"This is the only passage in a book of a thousand pages in which he even intimates that there were other children for his mother to take care of. No brother and no sister are mentioned in any other connection and even to his associate he has never admitted that there were other children besides his half-sister, Angela. Very little is said about his mother, either in writing or speaking. This concealment in itself would make one suspicious about the truth of the statement quoted above. One becomes even more suspicious when finding that not a single patient manifesting Hitler's character traits has grown up in such a well-ordered and peaceful home environment."[73]

In MEIN KAMPF Hitler gives a description of a child's life in a lower-class family. He says:

"Among the five children there is a boy, let us say, of three... When the parents fight almost daily, their brutality leaves nothing to the imagination; then the results of such visual education must slowly but inevitably become apparent to the little one. Those who are not familiar with such conditions can hardly imagine the results, especially when the mutual differences express themselves in the form of brutal attacks on the part of the father towards the mother or to assaults due to drunkenness. The poor little boy at the age of six senses thing which would make even a grown-up person shudder. The other things the little fellow hears at home do not tend to further his respect for his surroundings." [74]

Back to Mr. Langer's comments, "In view of the fact that there were five children in the Hitler home and that his father liked to spend his spare time in the village tavern where he sometimes drank so heavily that he had to be brought home by his wife or children, one may suspect that in this passage Hitler is probably describing conditions in his own home as a child." [75]

"If Hitler is actually talking about his own home when he describes conditions in the average lower-class family, one can obtain further information concerning the nature of his home environment:...things end badly indeed when the man from the very start goes his own way and the wife, for the sake of the children stands up against him. Quarreling and nagging set in, and in the same measure in which the husband becomes estranged from his wife, he becomes familiar with alcohol.....When he finally comes home... drunk and brutal, but always without a last cent or penny, then God have mercy on the scenes which follow. I witnessed all of this personally in hundreds of scenes and at the beginning with both disgust and indignation." [76]

To determine more about the Hitler family, look at Alois Jr. In 1910, a twenty-six year old Alois Jr. married an eighteen year old Irish woman named Bridget Dowling. By the next year they had a son, William Patrick Hitler. [77] Alois Jr. was known as a con man and gambling addict. He, as his father, consumed too much alcohol. [78] Alois Jr. would get drunk, beat Bridget, and then sought to do the same with his small son. Consequently his marriage failed, and he returned to Germany. [79] Bridget reared William Patrick alone. [80]

Adolf, who failed entry into art school, lost all means of support. [81] Adolf did not like to work, but would draw postcards to sell. In a downward spiral, a filthy Adolf Hitler lived a homeless life on the streets of Vienna before he joined the army. [82] While on the streets, he found shelter with a known homosexual Reinhold Hanisch. Adolf lived with him at a type of hotel known as a 'flophouse' which catered to the homosexual community. [83] Some think Adolf could have easily been involved in homosexual prostitution. He stayed in different flophouses and in the company of those who did. [84] [85] Also noted by Mr. Langer, "Adolf referred to one man, Foerster, as 'Bubi,' which was said to be a common nickname for a homosexual companion." [86] "More than one informant also spoke of Hitler's lack of sexual desire for women and his comfort around homosexuals." [87]

> "Mr. Langer believed Hitler was most probable 'impotent' in heterosexual relations and with Hitler's feminine characteristics, Mr. Langer believed he likely was involved in homosexuality."[88]

Another factor to consider came after Hitler's death is that an autopsy revealed a missing testicle.[89] Mr. Robert G. L Waite, who wrote the *Afterword* in *The Mind of Adolf Hitler*, established that "Adolf's behaviors were the same as pre-puberty boys with this condition that also had a history of behavioral disturbances."[90]

Other sexual antics of Adolf Hitler were his delight in pornography, gawking at nude women and male physics. Details of his delight in masochistic sexual degradation also came to light.[91] "One woman expected to have sex with Hitler, but instead, he begged to be repeatedly kicked and as she complied he groveled as unworthy of her presence."[92] Another reported of Adolf's coprophilous requests.[93] Such a request consisted of "having a woman urinate or defecate on him."[94] Adolf's niece, his sister Angela's daughter, Geli Raubal, reported this activity with her Uncle Adolf.

Just as Adolf's father Alois had done, Adolf turned the relationship with a niece into a sexual one. Adolf's jealousy and control of Geli literally made her his prisoner.[95] When she wanted out, Adolf kept someone with her to stop her.[96] The story goes that Geli sought to leave and marry, but Hitler found out, and the next day her body was found dead with Hitler's gun in her hand.[97] Ruled a suicide, but with much speculation over her death, many believed she was murdered.[98] Geli's description of Hitler's sexual demands provided vital information for the psychoanalysis done by the Office of Strategic Services (OSS). His so called love for Geli underlines the incestuous tendencies working in this family line. Out of the six female relationships in Adolf Hitler's life, two of them died of natural causes, and the others died as a consequence of suicide, or perhaps murder.[99]

Adolf's history is laced with sexual perversity. In his "twelfth year of high school, Adolf did something sexual to a little girl and was found guilty of sexual indiscretion." [100] "A couple of boys also reportedly identified themselves as Adolf's homosexual partners to Hermann Rauschnin."[101] Mr. Rauschning likewise gave a critical description concerning Hitler:

"Most loathsome of all is the reeking miasma of furtive, unnatural sexuality that fills and fouls the whole atmosphere around him, like an evil emanation." [102]

Another issue in Adolf's life came from excessive medicines given to him by Dr. Theodor Morell. Take note of all the different combinations of drugs; among them were highly addictive ones such as cocaine and pervatin (methamphetamine). In pictures Hitler looked like an old, frail man before he committed suicide, and these drugs contributed to his mental and physical condition.

Adolf feared smelling badly and took "huge amounts of anti-gas pills which contained strychnine and atrophene; since he feared obesity, he was given reducing pills of various sorts; since he suffered from nightmares and insomnia, he took at least a dozen different kinds of sleeping pills; because he feared impotency, Morell prescribed injections of pulverized bull testicles in grape sugar. He was also given massive doses of dexedrene, pervatin, caffeine, cocaine, prozymen and ultraseptyl as well as hugh amounts of vitamins." [103]

Hitler was known for tantrums and fits of rage which occurred when he did not get his way. On one hand, Adolf avoided making decisions, but once he did, anyone with a contradiction met his tirade. [104]Adolf, a tyrant in his own right, acted like his father, but as Führer, he could order death in a moments rage. [105]

Chapter 8

Hitler and the Occult Influence

"During questioning at the time of Geli's death, Hitler's told police of her involvement in a group that participated in séances where paranormal activity occurred. There Geli was told she would not die a natural death."[106] What stood out in Hitler's statement is that to him a séance with paranormal activity was normal. His thoughts that since Geli found out about an unnatural death, the police should accept that information as a pertinent factor in her death. To the average person, séances and tables moving are not normal, but to Hitler, it provided an acceptable reason for Geli's suicidal death and indicates a comfort in mentioning paranormal activity as a factor.

Adolf Hitler believed he was guided by providence, and occult activities laced Hitler's rise to power.[107] Occult is defined as "of or pertaining to magic, astrology, or any system claiming use or knowledge of secret or supernatural powers or agencies."[108]

The kingdom of Satan is the supernatural agency in occult activities which are forbidden by the Kingdom of God (Leviticus 19:31). As we work our way back in history, occult activity threads throughout the discovery process.

Chapter 9

Generational Transfers - Hitler Family Line

> We know our wickedness, O
> LORD, The iniquity of our
> fathers, for we have sinned
> against You. Jeremiah 14:20
> NASB

Numbers 14:18 provides insight on the
workings of sin and iniquity that moved
through the Hitler family line. There may be
more, but in this study we will focus on what is
obvious. Furthermore, we are dealing with
diabolical spirits working through sin nature
which are known by what they do or how they
manifest, so here we name them. We begin
with the man who fathered Alois Sr., and since
we do not know for sure which man did, we
have a dilemma. Alois was "illegitimate" as
stated on his birth certificate, so that is where
we begin. [109]

Recall Alois changed his name at age forty
years of age and asserted that Johann Georg
Hiedler was his biological father.[110] At that
time, Johann Georg Hiedler had already been

dead for two decades and while alive, neither he nor Maria ever claimed that Johann Georg's Hiedler (who married his mother) was Alois' biological father.[111] This is pertinent because Johann Georg's lineage would have ended without a male heir to carry on his name, so why would he not claim Alois if he truly was his son?

Alois used lies and deceit to get his last name changed. He provided three witnesses to a priest who did not know his mother or Johann Georg Hiedler. Johann Nepomuk Hiedler may have insisted on the name change. Once done, Alois became a male heir and carried the family name. This insistence to change his name at age forty could have simply been the way for Alois to claim the Hiedler inheritance.

Maria Schicklgruber's family lived as peasants for generations in an area in lower Austria known for obstinate, inflexible, and unreceptive people, which provides some insight.[112] Her parents had eleven children and only six survived to adulthood. It is unknown at this point if any illegitimate children existed in this family. As a note, mental illness ran in the Schicklgruber side of the family line. Aloisia Veit, a second cousin once removed from Adolf Hitler, was killed in a gas chamber due to the program which euthanatized the handicapped.[113] Her diagnosis of "schizophrenia, depression, delusions and other mental problems condemned her." [114] [115] This side of the family line came from Maria's aunt (her mother's sister) who died out due to mental illness and suicide. [116] Now we can add mental illness and suicide at work through the Schickgruber side of the family line. In viewing this history, one can surmise that all three of these mental illnesses transferred through the generations. Alois lived with his mother for his first ten years and would have observed her lifestyle. He probably witnessed immorality and physical aggression. Alois had a strong appetite for immorality, alcohol, and aggression towards others. Maria became involved with Johann Georg. In some accounts he moved in with her before they married, so a good probability existed for immorality yet again. [117] [118]

Out of the three men historically named as a possible father of Alois, all of them provided some type of financial benefit to Maria and/or Alois. Financial support came from Maria's ex-employer at the time of her pregnancy, which may mean a possible biological connection to this Jewish family. [119] From Johann Nepomuk Hiedler came a place to live for Alois, along with an inheritance. The third man, Johann Georg Hiedler, married Maria and would have provided some kind of support while they reared Alois for five years. As noted, Alois yielded an inheritance from Hiedler as well. If Maria was having sex with multiple sex partners during the time she got pregnant, she might not have known for sure who the father was. Or maybe she did, but kept silent to receive any financial assistance offered her. If so, multiple sex partners were manipulated to her benefit. As such, this could be deception.

Alois' biological father, the first generation, impregnated a woman without being married to her, so he was immoral and kept his identity hidden. The same applies to Maria, his mother. If Alois' biological father was the married Johann Nepomuk Hiedler, one can add adultery to the list. So with what we know so far, sexual immorality had access to this family line through his father and mother in the first generation with a child conceived illegitimately and a possibility of adultery.

Johann Georg Hiedler, whose occupation of a "miller or a wandering miller's helper" provides a peek into what Johann Georg could have been like. With Johann Georg's marriage to Maria, he became the father figure and male role model for a young Alois. So what kind of men were millers in Germany back then?

Millers were said to be "generally, wealthy but of a very bad moral image and their reputation stood as those who were not always honest. As an example of their deceit, a miller would mix flour with sand or gypsum, which of course would add extra weight to the price of the product. They were considered to be highly immoral. The last statement is based on the fact that the mills were naturally located outside the village (outside of the fortification walls). It was at the miller's location that events took place which the village would not tolerate within its own walls (prostitution, gambling with excessive drinking and partying.)"120 With that information in mind, one sees this behavior in Alois Hitler's life and in his family line.

Iniquity visits the second generation, which would be Alois himself and the mothers of his children. Since we already covered their lives, I will list the sin and or iniquity that I see from Alois Sr: Sexual immorality (fornication, adultery), conception of child with a woman not his wife (twice), multiple sex partners, pedophilia, incest, tyranny, arrogance, controlling, totalitarian, pride, violence, cruelty, addiction (alcohol, sex), child abuse, wife abuse, animal abuse, lying and a deceiver. When Alois Hitler ignored his wife and family, he acted as if they did not exist, so he abandoned them. He perhaps became depressed (mental issues in the family line) after the failure of his farm and turned to excessive alcohol that drowned his sorrow. 121 If Alois in anyway beat any of his children, which led to their death, then murder could be at work. A little iniquity coincidence, Alois married his first wife (at the end of her life) for financial gain, and he lost financially when his farm failed at the end of his life.

Fanny Matzelsberger of the second generational line of mothers had an affair with Alois when he was still married to his first wife. She conceived their first child while not married to him, so Alois Jr. was illegitimate, just as his father had been. Through Fanny one sees immorality (adultery, fornication)and an illegitimate child.

Klara Pölzl, became the mother of the rest of Alois Hitler's children. Fanny figured out the type of relationship Alois had with Klara, so Fanny did not want Klara's rivalry. Klara was sent away but returned as their housekeeper once Fanny became ill. Alois revealed the type of relationship he had with Klara when she conceived an illegitimate child with him as well.[122] It does not look like Alois had any morals or sexual restraint because he kept repeating the same scenarios. In this maternal line there was incest and immorality (fornication, adultery) that also produced an illegitimate child.

To address the third generation, consider Alois Jr. a "charming" scammer who had been arrested for theft twice and served time in jail.[123] "While employed as a waiter, Alois Jr. dressed slick, in the latest fashion, down to a pearl hat pin. He used this style for a scam as a wealthy hotelier."[124] Alois Jr. met Bridget Dowling, whose parents obviously saw through him and greatly objected to the relationship, but they married and had a son nine months later. Alois Jr. returned to Germany and, once there, WWI broke out. No problem. He married a German woman while still married to Bridget who remained in England.[125] In Germany, an illegitimate son came from his second family. Alois Jr. did not financially provide for his first wife and child and basically abandoned them. With WWI in progress, Alois Jr. sent word of his death to deceive Bridget. He was caught and tried for bigamy, but Bridget allowed him to go free.[126] [127]

Iniquities and sin areas of Alois Jr. were sexual immorality, adultery, bigamy, lying, theft, deception (con), violence, wife abuse, child abuse, tyrant (to his family) addiction to gambling and alcohol, and abandonment of his family. Alois Jr. lost financial benefit from a failed business just as Alois did at farming. This looks to be an iniquity flow in the generations. With Alois Jr., we now have a third generation of the same types of iniquities working in this family line.

Angela Hitler (sister of Alois Jr.) married Leo Raubal and had three children, so the iniquity of immorality does not seem to appear in her life. Leo Raubal died in 1910, and Angela remarried some time later after the death of her first husband.[128]

Next, consider Adolf Hitler's life where iniquity found great opportunity: immorality, sexual perversion, homosexuality, pornography, sexual depravity, multiple sex partners, pedophilia, incest, prostitution, merciless, despotism, arrogance, pride, tyrant, tyranny, addiction, deception, con, lying, violence, murder, mass murder, manipulation, spiritually immoral, self-exalted as god, and occultism.

Alois Sr. and Alois Jr conned for personal gain, and maybe Maria, but Adolf conned millions on a national scale by hypnosis and mind control. [129]

Adolf's only full bloodied sister, Paula Hitler, never married. She wanted to marry Dr. Erwin Jekelius, but Adolf did not approve and had him arrested. Erwin later died as a result of captivity.[130]

We have three generations of the same types of life choices in this family line. Their choices gave access to demonic activity in their midst. With an individual, iniquity may shift but still be an offshoot of the same type of sin. With that in mind, let's look at some of the shifts and turns.

First generation was immorality in the form of fornication and possibly adultery that produced an illegitimate child. The second generation also engaged in sexual immorality in the forms of fornication and adultery, and then Alois added incest and most likely pedophilia. Third generation added bigamy, homosexuality, prostitution, masochistic sex, coprophilous tendencies, and masochistically derived sexual gratification, suicide, and mass-murder. Violence, tyrannical behavior, and deception gained opportunity to harm this family line, along with the other generations of those murdered.

The fourth generation would be the sons of Alois Jr., William Patrick Hitler and his half-brother, Heinz Hitler, along with Angela's children. Heinz Hitler, a Nazi, was captured and died in prison in 1942.[131] William Patrick Hitler sought to benefit from his despot uncle and did gain employment with his help. [132] William became dissatisfied and attempted to blackmail both his father and Uncle Adolf. On one hand, William was provided a job by his Uncle Adolf and then chose to publically malign him. [133] With good reason, William did not trust Uncle Adolf and left Germany for the United States with his mother. Once in the United States, William joined the U.S. Navy and served in WWII. After the war, he started a successful business, married, and had four sons. No signs of immorality occurred here as in previous generation. However, by his scheme of blackmail, William continued the deceptive work of a con (like his father, grandfather, and possibly his great grandparents). [134]

Remember Angela's daughter Geli died officially of suicide. Angela's remaining son and daughter both married, and each had a son.[135] Suicide was in the family line as mentioned, and this spirit of death ran full throttle through Adolf's life. Suicide operated against the women he got close to. Not only them, but Adolf Hitler took his own life, and at the same time his wife took hers.

Chapter 10

Hitler's DNA

DNA testing on Adolf Hitler's family line made the news, so we will use this information to take us further back in time. "Investigative efforts of journalist Jean-Paul Mulders and historian Marc Vermeeren located thirty-nine of Hitler's living relatives in Austria and the United States."[136] Their findings appeared in the *Knack,* a Belgium magazine.[137] This discovery made known Hitler's Jewish and African ancestry. Hitler and the Nazis set out to destroy both Jews and those of African descent.

By the use of genetic fingerprints from groups of chromosomes called haplogroups, identification of genetic backgrounds of different people can be achieved.[138] Let's look at these findings.

Hitler's dominant haplogroup, E1b1b, is relatively rare in Western Europe - but strongest in some 25 percent of Greeks and Sicilians, who apparently acquired the genes from Africa: Between 50 percent and 80 percent of North Africans share Hitler's dominant group, which is especially prevalent among in the Berber tribes of Morocco, Algeria and Tunisia, and Somalis.[139]

Haplogroup E1b1b1, which accounts for approximately 18 to 20 per cent of Ashkenazi and 8.6 per cent to 30 per cent of Sephardic Y-chromosomes, appears to be one of the major founding lineages of the Jewish population.[140] From North Africa, Hitler's prevalent haplogroup, E1b1b came out of the native African tribes of the Berbers, who carry the highest percentage of this haplogroup. The Berbers made up the majority of North Africans according to early historical records that go back thousands of years.[141] "In the seventh century A.D., Arabs forced Berber tribes from North Africa by conquest and these tribes moved to Morocco, Algeria, Tunisia, Libya and Egypt." [142] Of the three sons of Noah, Africa descended from Ham, and the Berber tribes specifically from the Canaanites.[143]

Adolf Hitler's second haplogroup, E1b1b1 could have come out of the Ashkenaz Jews. Ashkenazi Jews came from "Germany, France and Eastern Europe, and were also called German Jews." Sephardic Jews were from "Spain, Portugal, North Africa and the Middle East."[144] Sephardic or Spanish Jews lived in the Iberian Peninsula before the Spanish Inquisition which forced them to leave.[145][146]

"The Table of Nations in Genesis Chapter Ten lists *Ashkenaz*, who was Noah's great grandson, Japheth's grandson and Gomer's first son (Gen. 10:3, 1 Chronicles 1:6)." [147] "In rabbinic literature, Ashkenaz is believed to be the ancestor of the Germanic people, probably due to the similarity of the names Gomer with German. For this reason, Ashkenaz is the Medieval Hebrew name for Germany."[148] "Historical accounts from the time period of Abraham through the Kingdoms of Judea and Israel, then their exile to Babylon, migration to Spain, then to the Middle East and Mediterranean, represent primarily the Sephardic Jewish culture."[149]

Chapter 11

Polygamy at the Root

Marriage should be honored by
all, and the marriage bed kept
pure, for God will judge the
adulterer and all the sexually
immoral. Hebrews 13:4 NIV

We know immorality moved through the
Hitler family line, but of great interest is the
reason why the Ashkenazi and Sephardic
Jewish cultures separated. The explanation of
their separation follows:

"Ashkenazic and Sephardic Jews
represent two distinct
subcultures of Judaism. We are
all Jews and share the same
basic beliefs, but there are some
variations in culture and
practice. It's not clear when the
split began, but it has existed for
more than a thousand years,
because around the year 1000

C.E., Rabbi Gershom ben Judah issued an edict against polygamy that was accepted by Ashkenazim but not by Sephardim."[150]

The dividing issue between these two groups came as a matter of polygamy. Prior to the edict by Rabbi Gershom ben Judah, both groups accepted polygamy. What is polygamy? It occurs "when a person has more than one spouse and in particular, when a man marries more than one wife at the same time." [151] What happens in polygamy? A man engages in sex with multiple partners or has sex with more than one woman. What did Alois Sr. and Alois Jr do? Alois Sr. had sex with women when he was married to another, and Alois Jr. committed bigamy. Both men had children with more than one woman. So simply expressed, take away the word "marriage" and see this behavior duplicates itself in Hitler's generations. A path for these generational sins and spirits can be seen through this family line and can be traced to these haplogroup. Immoral sex provides a spiritual door of admission to the body and can be used by the spiritual kingdom of darkness to gain access to a person's life (1 Corinthians 6:13b-20). This is covered in greater details in my book *Living with the Nephilim, the Seed of Destruction.* For the most part, Berbers do not practice polygamy, but it does exist among them today.[152]

From Satan's kingdom, territorial spirits exist over a nation and work to keep people transgressing in a particular manner. With that in mind, after the Thirty Year's War (1618–1648), Germany's parliament in 1650 permitted a man to marry as many as ten women due to the death of men killed in the war. I understand the reasoning, but this gave spiritual entrance to the generations of those who participated.[153] Similiarly, legislation in consideration for Germany for after WWII would have allowed a war hero to marry a second wife. [154]

Historically polygamy has religious connections, so let's define religion as "belief in, worship of, or obedience to a supernatural power or powers considered to be divine or to have control of human destiny." [155] Either in the past or present, polygamy can be found in a variety of religions. Some governments have also sanctioned polygamy, which generally ties to the religious views of a nation or its people. [156]

Chapter 12

Further Back in Time

The connection by DNA to the Berbers and Jews took us to North Africa. So back to history to find out when the Berbers and Jews could have interbred. "Early in Roman times, Moroccan Jews by way of Phoenician merchants began to trade with nomadic Berber tribes in remote areas near the Atlas Mountains."[157] At some point, the Jews decided to settle by the Berbers. Once they did, Jews and Berbers interbred.[158] These two groups of people blended commercially and culturally over the centuries, as they dressed the same and spoke the same Berber dialects.[159] Their religious beliefs also blended with some Berbers acceptance of Judaism, and various Jews practiced Berber mystical beliefs in saints, witchdoctors, and other occult practices which still exist among the Berbers.[160] "Berbers tribes of today depict their varying racial mixtures with diversity in skin colors, heights, builds and facial features."[161]

"Through Moroccan Berbers, a genealogical connection links their Canaanite heritage to a famous Philistine named Goliath."[162] [163] "A pre-king David slew a chief named 'Jalut,' also believed to be the Biblical giant known as Goliath."[164] "Upon the death of Goliath, the predecessors of the Berbers fled Palestine and became scattered throughout North Africa."[165] Canaan was the land originally settled by Canaan, the youngest son of Ham. In Biblical events the land of Canaan was given to the nation of Israel by a promise from God to Abraham (Genesis 15:18-21). Moses led Israel out of Egypt (Exodus 12), and Joshua led them into the Canaan Land (Book of Joshua). Not only is there a Jew and Berber connection but add the Canaanites and a certain Philistine. Now consider the ancient culture of the Egyptians.

After the Flood of Noah

Chapter 13

The Egyptians

The patriarch of the Egyptians, Philistines, Canaanites, and the Phoenicians goes back to Ham, the son of Noah. Ham exposed his heart which was set in rebellion to authority and toward sexual immorality. His actions toward his father in Genesis 9:20-24 made this clear. From Ham's son Mizraim the Egyptians came forth and a glance at their lifestyles gives a good overview of this family line.

> The sons of Ham were Cush and Mizraim and Put and Canaan. Genesis 10:6 NASB

> 13 Mizraim became the father of Ludim and Anamim and Lehabim and Naphtuhim 14 and Pathrusim and Casluhim (from which came the Philistines) and Caphtorim. Genesis 10:13-18 NASB

15 Canaan became the father of Sidon, his firstborn, and Heth 16 and the Jebusite and the Amorite and the Girgashite 17 and the Hivite and the Arkite and the Sinite 18 and the Arvadite and the Zemarite and the Hamathite; and afterward the families of the Canaanite were spread abroad. Genesis 10:15-18 NASB

Since Mizraim begat the Egyptians, his children were Egyptians, who in turn became progenitors of others. The Philistines also connect their heritage to Ham through Mizraim, who conquered land and lived near their Canaanites relatives (Deuteronomy 2:23, 1 Chronicles 1:12, Jeremiah 47:4). Mizraim's sons Casluhim and Caphtorim had descendants on the island of Crete where the Philistines originated.[166]

11 Mizraim became the father of the people of Lud, Anam, Lehab, Naphtuh, 12 Pathrus, Casluh, from which the Philistines came, and Caphtor. 1 Chronicles 1:11 NASB

To continue this backward march in time, one needs to understand the culture of the ancient Egyptians, Canaanites, and the Philistines.

Ancient Egyptian culture focused on the worship of mythological gods and life after death by obtaining eternal life through meticulous burial rituals. The Egyptians were led by Pharaohs who believed they and theirs were significant enough to gain entry to the land of eternal life, and those of no importance would not gain such entry.[167] Pharaohs played an important role in their beliefs, but over time, this changed.

"Formal religious practice centered on the Pharaoh, the king of Egypt. Although human, the Pharaoh was believed to be descended from the gods. He acted as the intermediary between his people and the gods and was obligated to sustain the gods through rituals and offerings so that they could maintain order in the universe. Therefore, the state dedicated enormous resources to the performance of these rituals and to the construction of the temples where these rituals were carried out. Individuals could also interact with the gods for their own purposes, appealing for their help through prayer or compelling them to act through magic."[168] In this quest, they built pyramids, embalmed and mummified the dead, left grave supplies for the journey to the afterlife, cast magic spells, and used charms for luck.[169]

Egyptian sexuality of this time period appears familiar. Prostitutes wore tattoos, loud makeup, and advertised their wares through scanty attire. [170] No guilt existed for one's sexuality, as the unmarried male or female chose many partners. [171] In a marriage, adultery was not accepted and could be punished by death. Women bore the most severe penalties compared to males. When it came to the elites, such as a Pharaoh, he had many wives.[172] To the Egyptians, child bearing provided a source of pride to one's fertility, but alongside childbirth, Egyptian developed birth control and abortion.[173] According to their belief, sex was not only for earthly enjoyment but for the afterlife.[174] The gods of the Egyptians were sexually perverse role models for the Egyptian population as they glorified "immorality, incest, homosexuality, masturbation and necrophilia. [175] One of their gods, Hapi, had both male and female attributes as a hermaphrodite. Two other gods, Set and Horus, engaged in homosexual acts together, while another depicted an act of male masturbation.

Incest was common in Egypt, especially in the royal family of the Pharaohs. To become a Pharaoh, a male had to marry a princess of royal bloodline. Since they believed the royal bloodline passed only from a female, a brother would marry his sister or a parent would marry the offspring.[176] This became their custom since Egyptian gods participated in sibling marriages. They sought to strengthen such bonds to their gods by doing the same.[177]

These practices of the Egyptians and Canaanite cultures were forbidden by God of the Bible in a detailed list found in Leviticus, Chapter 18. Was God keeping his people from having fun? Not at all. He sought to keep his children from sin and the human misery such actions caused.

> You must not do as they do in Egypt, where you used to live, and you must not do as they do in the land of Canaan, where I am bringing you. Do not follow their practices. Leviticus 18:3 NIV

Chapter 14

Canaanites

Canaan became the father of eleven sons and his first born, Sidon, established the city of Sidon and became the ancestor of the Phoenicians.[178] Just as with the Egyptians, God warned his children not to imitate the Canaanites. The Canaanites, like the Egyptians, engaged in spiritism (occult practices) which was forbidden by God. They also offered their children as human sacrifices.

> Spiritism Forbidden - 9 "When you enter the land which the Lord your God gives you, you shall not learn to imitate the detestable things of those nations. 10 There shall not be found among you anyone who makes his son or his daughter pass through the fire, one who uses divination, one who practices witchcraft, or one who interprets omens, or a sorcerer, 11 or one who casts a spell, or a

medium, or a spiritist, or one who calls up the dead. 12 For whoever does these things is detestable to the LORD; and because of these detestable things the LORD your God will drive them out before you. 13 You shall be blameless before the Lord your God. 14 For those nations, which you shall dispossess, listen to those who practice witchcraft and to diviners, but as for you, the Lord your God has not allowed you to do so." Deuteronomy 18:9-14 NASB

Leviticus Chapter 18 lists sexual practices of these people and God warned against them. First off, "do not approach any relative to 'uncover their nakedness' which means to have sexual relationships; not your father, mother, sister, brother, half siblings, aunts, uncles, sons, daughters any kind of in-laws, not anyone of kin, it is wickedness" (Leviticus 18:6-18).

6 No one is to approach any close relative to have sexual relations. I am the LORD. Leviticus 18:6 NIV

Additional sexual practices warned against.

> 20 "Do not have sexual relations with your neighbor's wife and defile yourself with her. 21Do not give any of your children to be sacrificed to Molech, for you must not profane the name of your God. I am the LORD. 22 Do not lie with a man as one lies with a woman; that is detestable. 23 Do not have sexual relations with an animal and defile yourself with it. A woman must not present herself to an animal to have sexual relations with it; that is a perversion." Leviticus 18:20-23 NIV

Clearly, these practices were done by both the Egyptians and Canaanites as stated in Leviticus 28:27.

> ...for all these things were done by the people who lived in the land before you, and the land became defiled. Leviticus 18:27 NIV

Canaanite and Egyptians religious customs were influenced by ancient Mesopotamian polytheism.[179] Their lives evolved around appeasement of their gods for everyday needs and the quest for eternal life. Along with household gods, they worshipped others such as Baal, El, and Asherah, who was considered to be mother earth. [180] One aspect of the Canaanites, Phoenicians, Babylonians, and other nations in this region was the use of male and female prostitution in acts of worship to their gods.[181] Greek historian Herodotus provided his thought on ancient Mesopotamians temple prostitution. [182] This cultural practice gave demonic access to every female in their society through immoral sexual intercourse, which allowed sexual iniquity to visit the next generations.

> The foulest Babylonian custom is that which compels every woman of the land to sit in the temple of Aphrodite and have intercourse with some stranger once in her life. Many women who are rich and proud and disdain to mingle with the rest, drive to the temple in covered carriages drawn by teams, and stand there with a great retinue of attendants. But most sit down in the sacred plot of Aphrodite, with crowns of cord on their heads; there is a great

multitude of women coming and going; passages marked by line run every way through the crowd, by which the men pass and make their choice. Once a woman has taken her place there, she does not go away to her home before some stranger has cast money into her lap, and had intercourse with her outside the temple; but while he casts the money, he must say, "I invite you in the name of Mylitta" (that is the Assyrian name for Aphrodite). It does not matter what sum the money is; the woman will never refuse, for that would be a sin, the money being by this act made sacred. So she follows the first man who casts it and rejects no one. After their intercourse, having discharged her sacred duty to the goddess, she goes away to her home; and thereafter there is no bribe however great that will get her. So then the women that are fair and tall are soon free to depart, but the uncomely have long to wait because they cannot fulfill the law.[183]

These people also engaged in an *Ancient Fertility Rite* which involved sex acts, intoxication, and human sacrifice. [184] After Israel moved into the land of Canaan, they ignored what they were warned about and became just like them.

> Then the sons of Israel again did evil in the sight of the LORD, served the Baals and the Ashtaroth, the gods of Aram, the gods of Sidon, the gods of Moab, the gods of the sons of Ammon, and the gods of the Philistines; thus they forsook the LORD and did not serve Him. Judges 10:6 KJV

Why would the Israelites have trouble heeding these warnings? Their ancestors grew up in Egypt and generational iniquity worked to ensure access to their lives.

Chapter 15

Philistine Giants

Not much difference existed in the culture and practices of the Philistine from their Egyptian, Canaanite, and Greek neighbors, as the worship of pagan gods flourished. "Archeology provides insight into the Philistines from ancient Ashkelon; with findings such as burial artifacts of magic charms like those used by the Egyptian, remains of what were large, well-built men (confirmation of size) and a ditch with tiny skeletal remains of dozens of newborn babies, tossed out as trash (indicates no human value given to these babies)."[185] Pottery displayed sexual practices of their culture that included homosexuality like those practices found in Egypt. [186]

However, one thing differed: the Philistines produced strong drink and consumed alcoholic beverages.[187] "In anthropological digs, items used to produce, store, advertise, sell and consume alcoholic beverage have been found. If beer, wine or stronger alcohol was desired, the Philistines provided the goods."[188]

Additionally, among discovered artifacts was Philistine pottery that exalted a well-known ancient giant named Goliath. [189] Goliath was the giant Moroccan Berbers claimed as their ancestor (1 Samuel 17:4-7; 23). When Joshua led Israel into Canaan, Israel defeated the Anakim, a tribe of giants who descended from a giant named Anak.[190]

21 Then Joshua came at that time and cut off the Anakim from the hill country, from Hebron, from Debir, from Anab and from all the hill country of Judah and from all the hill country of Israel. Joshua utterly destroyed them with their cities. 22 There were no Anakim left in the land of the sons of Israel; only in Gaza, in Gath, and in Ashdod some remained. Joshua 11:21-22 NASB

Hebron stood as a city built seven years before Zoan Egypt and was known as the city of Arba, whose offspring were a lineage of giants.

Now the name of Hebron was
formerly Kiriath-arba; for Arba
was the greatest man among the
Anakim. Then the land had rest
from war. Joshua 14:15 NASB

Defining Hebron by the Hebrew word,
chebrown along with its root word *chebe*, offers
a clue to the practices of those in ancient
Hebron. This definition of "an association, or
society of magicians, charmers and spiritists,"
confirms the same activities as the people
studied so far. [191] [192] Arba would have been
conceived after the flood and may be one of the
first of the giants born then. This certainly
could be possible, since Hebron, the city he
founded, became a place of organized occult
activity after the flood.

Arba became the father of Anak who had
three sons, which would be the third
generation of giants from this family line. By
the time of King David, Arba's fourth
generation was alive on earth. So Arba's
genetics transferred from one generation to the
next along with the same behaviors. Other
giants existed, but Arba was said to be the
greatest of the giants (Anakim).[193] Arba may
have been the most renowned wizard,
magician, or spiritist among the giants in
Hebron. Wherever there are giants, there will
be occult activity.

10 The Emim lived there formerly, a people as great, numerous, and tall as the Anakim. 11 Like the Anakim, they are also regarded as Rephaim, but the Moabites call them Emim. Deuteronomy 2:10-11 NASB

Chapter 16

Goliath, the Nephilim Giant

⁴And a champion went out of the camp of the Philistines named Goliath of Gath, whose height was six cubits and a span [almost ten feet]. ⁵And he had a bronze helmet on his head and wore a coat of mail, and the coat weighed 5,000 shekels of bronze. ⁶He had bronze shin armor on his legs and a bronze javelin across his shoulders.⁷And the shaft of his spear was like a weaver's beam; his spear's head weighed 600 shekels of iron. And a shield bearer went before him. 1 Samuel 17:4-7 Amplified Bible

When battle lines had been drawn between the Philistines and Israelites, Goliath stepped out from the Philistine ranks and demanded a man to do hand to hand combat with him (1 Samuel 17:1-10).

10And the Philistine said, I defy the ranks of Israel this day; give me a man, that we may fight together.11When Saul and all Israel heard those words of the Philistine, they were dismayed and greatly afraid. 1 Samuel 17:10-11 Amplified Bible

Not only did Goliath demand a man to do hand to hand combat with him once, but every day, morning and evening for forty days. A youthful David heard his taunt and took the challenge (1 Samuel 17:14).

23As they talked, behold, Goliath, the champion, the Philistine of Gath, came forth from the Philistine ranks and spoke the same words as before, and David heard him. 24And all the men of Israel, when they saw the man, fled from him, terrified. 1 Samuel 17:23-24 Amplified Bible

What was the result of the giant Goliath's presence? Men became "dismayed and greatly afraid." (1 Samuel 17:11) The word *dismayed* means "to break down the courage completely, as by sudden danger or trouble; dishearten thoroughly." [194] He not only took their courage, but he filled them with terror. Goliath was a bully, a tyrant, a terrorist. He was a giant and a descendant of a giant.

> And unto Caleb the son of Jephunneh he gave a part among the children of Judah, according to the commandment of the Lord to Joshua, [even] the city of Arba the father of Anak, which [city is] Hebron. And Caleb drove thence the three sons of Anak, Sheshai, and Ahiman, and Talmai, the children of Anak. Joshua 15:13-14 KJV

We read of more giants in the city of Gath, Goliath's home town.

> 4 Now it came about after this, that war broke out at Gezer with the Philistines; then Sibbecai the Hushathite killed Sippai, one of the descendants of the giants, and they were subdued.

5 And there was war with the Philistines again, and Elhanan the son of Jair killed Lahmi the brother of Goliath the Gittite, the shaft of whose spear was like a weaver's beam. 6 Again there was war at Gath, where there was a man of great stature who had twenty-four fingers and toes, six fingers on each hand and six toes on each foot; and he also was descended from the giants. 7 When he taunted Israel, Jonathan the son of Shimea, David's brother, killed him. 8 These were descended from the giants in Gath, and they fell by the hand of David and by the hand of his servants. 1 Chronicles 20:4-8 NASB Forty years before Joshua led Israel into the Canaan land; Israelite spies saw the sons of Anak and identified them as the Nephilim. As a giant from Gath, Goliath descended from Anak, and by the description of these spies, the sons of Anak were giants known as Nephilim (Numbers 13:32).

32 So they gave out to the sons of Israel a bad report of the land which they had spied out, saying, "The land through which we have gone, in spying it out, is a land that devours its inhabitants; and all the people whom we saw in it are men of *great* size. 33 "There also we saw the Nephilim (the sons of Anak are part of the Nephilim); and we became like grasshoppers in our own sight, and so we were in their sight" Numbers 13:32 NASB.

From here, one must understand the Nephilim.

Before the Flood of Noah

Chapter 17

The Nephilim

The next stop on the journey back in time will be Genesis, the first book of the Bible to find out about the Nephilim.

> 1 Now it came about, when men began to multiply on the face of the land, and daughters were born to them, 2 that the sons of God saw that the daughters of men were beautiful; and they took wives for themselves, whomever they chose. 4The Nephilim were on the earth in those days, and also afterward, when the sons of God came in to the daughters of men, and they bore children to them. Those were the mighty men who were of old, men of renown. Genesis 6:1-2, 4 NASB

The existence of the Nephilim and how they came about were revealed in this scripture. Sons of God bred daughters of men, and their offspring were called Nephilim. The Nephilim were not referred to as men in the first part of Genesis 6:4 but lived on earth alongside men. They interbred with daughters of men and blended with humans to the point they were called men. We need to understand these particular sons of God, and what they wanted on planet earth.

In Genesis 6, sons of God were angels, called as watchers over mankind, but these angels rebelled against their God's ordained place. They took the form of human men in order to do one main thing: have sex and a lot of it.[195] They sought to produce offspring with any female they chose. As angels in rebellion to the Most High God, they were fallen angels which we call devils. Laws and ordinances set by God stood ignored by these angels, so they released abnormalities into human genetics. Some may think this is impossible, but scripturally angels do take human form (Genesis 19:1). Some people have been around angels and did not know, because angels have the ability to look like humans.[196]

Do not neglect to show
hospitality to strangers, for by
this some have entertained
angels without knowing it.
Hebrews 13:2 NASB

Sons of God who bred with daughters of
men created evil offspring for Satan, which
God told Eve would occur.

14 Then the Lord God said to the
serpent ... And I will cause
hostility between you and the
woman, and between your
offspring and her offspring. He
will strike your head, and you
will strike his heel." Genesis
3:14-15 NLT

Eve blamed the serpent when she
disobeyed the command from God. "And the
woman said, 'The serpent deceived me, and I
ate.'" (Genesis 3:15). A normal serpent could
not deceive, but the spirit that operated
through the serpent could and that spirit was
Satan. The war that began in heaven came to
earth. Eve understood Satan would have
offspring alongside hers and because of them,
there would be ongoing hostility. Satan's plan
to destroy men and their families began once
Adam sinned. Fallen angels were able to gain
access to humans through their sin nature.

Then the next phase began when a satanic
bred of humans arose through the
Nephilim.

Chapter 18

Nephilim Understood

A breakdown of three descriptive phrases for the Nephilim reveals pertinent information as described in my book, *Living with the Nephilim, the Seed of Destruction.*

> 4 The Nephilim (giants) were on the earth in those days, and also afterward, when the sons of God came in to the daughters of men, and they bore children to them. Those were the mighty men who were of old, men of renown. Genesis 6:4 KJV

The Hebrew word "gibbowr" (Strongs #1368) for "**mighty men**," first appears in Genesis 6:4, defined as powerful. By implication, this translates to warrior, tyrant - champion, chief, excel, giant, man.[197]

The next phrase for Nephilim, "**who were of old**" from *(Strongs #5769)*, a Hebrew word "olam" meaning "what is hidden, of time long past, perpetuity, concealed, i.e. the vanishing point; with a short definition, of "forever" or "eternity."[198] Sons of God and their offspring would possess origins from the spirit world or eternity.

`*Alam* (**Strong's H 5956**) the Hebrew root word for `*Owlam* gives more details to grasp just what we are dealing with concerning the Nephilim. `*Alam* means to conceal, hide, be hidden, be concealed, be secret, to hide oneself, dissembler.[199] Now to define dissemble: 1) to give a false or misleading appearance; to conceal the truth or real nature of; 2) to conceal one's true motives, thoughts, etc., by some pretense; speak or act hypocritically. Next add synonyms for dissemble: mask, hide, camouflage. Now we discover how the Nephilim act in our midst. [200]

The last phrase "**men of renown**" reveals the Nephilim were known or famous, which can be understood by one of three Hebrew words for Nephilim, *naphal,* meaning "a feller, a bully or a tyrant - giant." [201] Nephilim became famous because they were fellers, bullies, and tyrants. [202] Feller defined is "fierce, cruel; dreadful, destructive; deadly, savage, along with synonyms of barbaric, unrestrained, inhuman and inhumane to name a few that indicates what they were like. [203] [204] A bully is a "quarrelsome, overbearing person who habitually badgers and intimidates smaller or weaker people." [205] A tyrant is "any person in a position of authority who exercises power oppressively or despotically." [206] "In the exact sense, a tyrant arrogates to him or herself royal authority without having a right to it. This is how the Greeks understood the word 'tyrant'."[207] This definition brings out the elitism of the Nephilim in their minds. Another term for a tyrant is a dictator, or the means by which these people seize power.[208]

Tyrants and bullies seek control; God gave man liberty to make his own life choices. Not so with Nephilim. They want to control others and make them subject to them. Nephal, singular for Nephilim, means "a living abortion."[209] Along with terminating a pregnancy, abortion can mean a monstrous person.[210] The Nephilim are living monsters and, interestingly, a monster is a super natural being and the essence of this problem.[211]

Chapter 19

Biblical Origins

Psychopaths came about when sons of God bred with daughters of men. With Nephilim origins of one part human and one part fallen angel in the form of a human male, I believe Nephilim genetics produce psychopaths. When sons of God intruded into mankind, Satan gained his own seed of humans, made in his image and likeness with the Nephilim. Satan himself is the utlimate psychopath.

> For you are the children of your father the devil and you love to do the evil things he does. He was a murderer from the beginning. He has always hated the truth, because there is no truth in him. When he lies, it is consistent with his character; for he is a liar and the father of lies. John 8:44 NLT

Then he said, "You son of the devil, full of every sort of deceit and fraud, and enemy of all that is good! Acts 13:10 NLT a

As Nephilim descendants interbred with humans, they eventually looked like any other person as scripture called them men (Genesis 6:4).

4The Nephilim were on the earth in those days, and also afterward, when the sons of God came in to the daughters of men, and they bore children to them. **Those were the mighty men** who were of old, men of renown. Genesis 6:4 KJV

The Nephilim were among the general population, but most people were not Nephilim. However, the rest of earth's population transgressed when they became like the Nephilim and were corrupted. This gave these unclean spirits access to the population of all the earth. We know this happened as Noah was the only one found righteous prior to the flood. After the flood, a two-fold Nephilim assault continued against mankind: one from man's physical genetics passed down from a family line and the other from spirits of wickedness that accompany these family lines. Satan did not change his tactics but sent out breeders again to release genetic corruption into the normal population of humans.

> The Nephilim were on the earth in those days, **and also afterward**, when the sons of God came in to the daughters of men, and they bore children to them. Genesis 6:4 a NASB

From the invisible world, spirits of devils and demons would work to entice humans to sin just as they did before the flood and thus gain spiritual entry into more humans and their family lines. Satan would use the Nephilim to greatly debase life on earth as before the flood.

Nephilim were satanic seed born out of rebellion and became agents of immorality. While pondering this, think about Nephilim sperm: it could not produce normal humans. In any study on psychopaths, there is a difference between them and others who display the same behaviors. Biblically a difference existed between Nephilim and other men who committed the same evil behaviors. This shines the light on Cain in the murder of his brother Able. Cain was not a Nephilim, but a man tempted to do evil. Cain's temptation came from sin crouching at the door of his heart. Genesis 4: 6 and 7 reveals a Spirit to spirit conversation as God, a Spirit, explains sin's enticement and plan to use Cain for evil.

> 6"Why are you so angry?" the Lord asked Cain. "Why do you look so dejected? 7You will be accepted if you do what is right. But if you refuse to do what is right, then watch out! Sin is crouching at the door, eager to control you. But you must subdue it and be its master."8One day Cain suggested to his brother, "Let's go out into the fields." And while they were in the field, Cain attacked his brother, Abel, and killed him. Genesis 4:6-8 NLT

> If thou doest well, shalt thou not be accepted? and if thou doest not well, sin lieth at the door. And unto thee [shall be] **his** desire, and thou shalt rule over **him**. Genesis 4:6b KJ

In this sentence, sin connects to the word *it*, but in the King James translation the word *it* translates as *him*. A *he* desired to have Cain, the *he* was a spirit that could crouch and wait. In this Biblical account, sin sat at the door of Cain's heart. An evil spirit stayed with Cain to seize him for its purpose, "sin is crouching at the door, eager to control you" (Genesis 4:6.). This illustrates how an evil spirit tempts people to give in to sin or iniquity from their family line. The scripture in 1 Corinthians 7:5 explains that Satan is the spirit behind temptation.

> Stop depriving one another, except by agreement for a time, so that you may devote yourselves to prayer, and come together again so that Satan will **not tempt you** because of your lack of self-control. 1 Corinthians 7:5 NASB

History and modern times tell the stories of atrocities by people who lack what normal humans possess because they are not normal and cannot be because of their origins. This not only occurred in the nations mentioned in the Bible but by migration. Nephilim genetics moved throughout the generations and all over earth.

Chapter 20

Spiritual Maneuvering

Nephilim reproduced genetically and culturally prior to the flood of Noah. Today we know psychopaths do genetically and culturally reproduce as well. The twin study pointed to the hereditary and social environments behind psychopathy. [212] To this information add another spiritual component. From the spirit realm, a spiritual maneuvering can occur to bring people together. An example of this took place when Aaron met his brother Moses in the wilderness.

> 18Then Moses departed and returned to Jethro his father-in-law and said to him, "Please, let me go, that I may return to my brethren who are in Egypt, and see if they are still alive." And Jethro said to Moses, "Go in peace." 19Now the LORD said to Moses in Midian, "Go back to Egypt, for all the men who were seeking your life are dead." 20So

Moses took his wife and his sons
and mounted them on a donkey,
and returned to the land of
Egypt. Moses also took the staff
of God in his hand. 27Now the
LORD said to Aaron, "Go to meet
Moses in the wilderness." So he
went and met him at the
mountain of God and kissed him.
Exodus 4:18-20; 27 NASB

God began to direct Moses when he
lived in Midian. Remember no cell phones
or texting existed. God, a Spirit, told
Aaron in Egypt to go into the desert and
meet his brother Moses. Scripture clearly
informs us of what happened. "So he
(Aaron) went and met him (Moses) at the
mountain of God and kissed him" (Exodus
4:27). Wow, no problem for God. From the
spirit realm, they were brought together
for holy purposes. Their meeting did not
come about any other way.

Similarly, if God brings people
together for his purposes, the satanic
kingdom does also. Evil spirits work in
family lines to entice iniquity, such as
with King David's children. Those with
Nephilim heritage along with their
accompanying spirits get together for sex
to produce more of these people. This
ensures that Satan will continue to have
his seed available for use. Psychopaths

make it easy for him. I believe many come together by spiritual maneuvering of iniquity's evil forces. These spirits are also at work to create situations for sexual contact, such as in rape or pedophilia. The goal is sexual contact which creates a physical and spiritual joining for their use.

Chapter 21

Altered Humans

There are different classifications of prehistoric humans with criteria determined by men. Biblically we need to understand they came about by the intrusion of angels against God's order (Genesis 6:4). Darwinism, in its theory of evolution, does not take this truth into account. I believe physical evidence proves the Biblical account of these altered species of humans that existed along with the descendants of Adam and Eve.

Over time different terms have been used to classify humans based on archaeological discovery. Members from the original group of humans, which I call Adam's seed, migrated and interbred with a species of humans called the Neanderthals. This began in the Middle East region and probably North Africa.[213] Neanderthals by classification are called a subspecies of homo sapiens (*homo sapiens neanderthalensis*) or a separate human species (*homo neanderthalensis*).[214] Some believe they totally became extinct, but in reality they inbred and migrated throughout Europe and into southwestern and central Asia and thus blended in. By interbreeding with Adam's seed they merged into the human populations. Biblically, Genesis 6:4 is the scripture that clearly states their existence and the source of their origins. The Biblical terminology given to them was Nephilim or giants.

Various Neanderthal archeological finds have been discovered from Europe to Asia. [215] In 1856 the first remains of a Neanderthal were found in a cave, ironically by a pastor, in Germany. The Neanderthal discoveries in Germany and Europe provide evidence that Nephilim were alive and bred in the region of Hitler's ancestors. [216]

Chapter 22

Ham's Choice

Our trail led us to the patriarch Ham, whose behavior, along with his children and grandchildren's behavior, revealed a lot. The Nephilim presence affected everyone, even those who entered the ark. We know Noah was perfect in his generation (Genesis 6:9), and scriptures says this of no one else on the ark. We also know Noah led his family in line with God's commands, which saved their lives.

Noah and his three sons found wives before the flood because they all entered the ark. These women greatly influenced the outcome of their offspring, just like their fathers. Take note: Noah's family lived about Nephilim cultures. Once off the ark, all three of Noah's sons moved on to lead their families in accordance with their own ways of life.

Ham exposed his heart and lifestyle choice when he fixed his eyes upon his father's nakedness. He did not honor his father Noah. His actions were the ways of the Nephilim

(Genesis 9:21-23). Through Ham, a heart of rebellion arose against God (who Noah represented) along with sexual immorality which encompassed incest and perversion. These iniquities transferred to subsequent generations which included the Egyptians, Canaanites, Phoenicians, and the Philistines.

What about Ham's wife? The children she nurtured and they reared provide a glimpse about her. I believe Ham's wife also embraced Nephilim culture. These transgressions had a firm grip on Ham's descendants. As someone with Nephilim ideologies, Ham's wife most likely passed these on to her family. These would have been paganism, along with witchcraft and other occult practices that accompany those who accept them. Their descendants worshipped sexually perverted and immoral gods, who were said to have bred with humans and created god men. These gods sought to be worshipped and required human sacrifices to appease them. All these cultural components were a carryover of the pre-flood practices of the Nephilim. Not only did Ham's lineage come under the influence of the Nephilim culture, eventually so did descendants of both his brothers. Nephilim culture demands acceptance of sexual and spiritual immoralities. With that said, these sins transferred to their descendants.

Chapter 23

Spiritual Power of Sex

7And the LORD God formed man of the dust of the ground, and breathed into his nostrils the breath of life; and man became a living soul. Genesis 2:7 KJV

As we know, any male can have sex with any female and reproduce if the physical anatomy is working correctly. Due to Satan's determination in corrupting Adam's seed, Moses provided the details of God's protection plan.

21And the Lord God caused a deep sleep to fall upon Adam, and he slept: and he took one of his ribs, and closed up the flesh instead thereof; 22And the rib, which the Lord God had taken from man, made he a woman, and brought her unto the man.23And Adam said, This is now bone of my bones, and flesh of my flesh: she shall be called Woman, because she was taken out of Man. [24]Therefore shall a man leave his father and his mother, and shall cleave unto his wife: and they shall be one flesh. [25]And they were both naked, the man and his wife, and were not ashamed. Genesis 2:21-25 KJV

When Moses shared God's creation of the first man and woman, he revealed the marriage covenant. God took a part of the first man and placed it in his woman. In this first surgery, God used Adam's rib and "made he a woman" (Genesis 2:22) and brought them together. Notice it was the work of God that made a woman for a man, and it was God's work that brought them together. She was "bone of his bone and flesh of his flesh." She was his match; she was a female him (Genesis 2:23). They were united to God and created to be married.

God made man, male and female, and the breath of life from God filled them both. Scripture does not say God breathed into her nostrils the breath of life as He did with Adam We know this occurred, but the emphasis here reveals that an impartation of life came from the man into woman. Here is the close, intimate relationship God designed for marriage.

God's best was none other than one man and one woman, joined together by covenant. As a couple united by and to God, they became one physically and spiritually, which made a covenantal trinity meant to protect marriage. A person standing alone can be attacked and defeated, but two can stand back-to-back to overcome. Three are even better, for a triple-braided cord is not easily broken Ecclesiastes 4:12 NLT

Adam and Eve were not only the first man and wife, but the first couple that had sex. In Genesis, chapter two, God set precedence for sexual intimacy to take place in the marriage covenant. They not only bonded, but sex made them a family (Genesis 2:24). A man was designed to transfer life through sex which signaled he had cleaved and formed a family with his wife.

> Therefore shall a man leave his father and his mother, and shall cleave unto his wife: and they shall be one flesh. Genesis 2:24 KJV

Cleave means "to cling, stick, stay close, stay with, and join to." [217] A husband cleaves to and stays with the wife he joined by covenant and not another. Satan set out to destroy marriage to hinder or stop this powerful spiritual covenant intended to protect against his wiles. Not all are called to be married, and

God knows circumstances arise to end marriages. But God's best for marriage is to do so in his will and to stay that way. For many reasons, this does not always happen. Divorce makes a way for bad marriages to end and for people to begin a fresh start.

> And they were both naked, the man and his wife, and were not ashamed (Genesis 2:25).

This statement indicates shame is a human response when sex takes place outside the marriage covenant. "The word 'ashamed' focuses on the sense of one's own responsibility for an act, whether it is foolish, improper, or immoral."[218] Shame should normally be present in immorality which breaks the moral code placed in humans by our Creator (Hebrews 10:16). Married or not, sexual intercourse unites two people both physical and spiritually because of God's arrangement in creation.

In immoral sex, no covenant or bond of commitment legitimizes the union, just sexual gratification. One may feel he or she is good enough for sex but not marriage. Since Nephilim posterities exist without normal consciousness, they do not care about another's feelings. They choose immoral lifestyles to gratify their sexual desires. If they marry, cheating may take place.

When Adam and Eve broke their covenant of obedience to God's word, God first addressed Adam. Why? Adam was accountable to walk according to God's Word given to him. Adam was in charge, and what happened ultimately was his responsibility. God addressed Eve about what she did as well, and as an individual, she also was held accountable for her actions. However, it was disobedience to a command of God that released Satan and his forces against them (Genesis 2:16-17).

With this in mind, think about Alois Hitler's sexual activities, before, during, and in between his marriages. One could conclude they were marriages by paper, but no covenant of commitment and forsaking of all others existed. Alois' first marriage was a scheme to benefit him financially and aid his career. The second and third marriages came out of immorality and occurred to legitimize illegitimate children. His third marriage also provided him a needed babysitter for his young children.

The result? Alois did not honor marriage fidelity. He certainly could have, but he did not. Although the Hitlers were married, sin and iniquities left open doors for destructive spiritual forces to bring harm to their family.

We established that Nephilim genes move through family lines along with the same forms of Nephilim spirits. Prior immorality, or lack of morality, keeps doors open for these unclean spirits to continue iniquity in a family line. Understand those who do not embrace their lifestyles, but associate with these people, should watch out. Their spiritual entourages of unclean spirits seek opportunity to infect the lives of others.

> Do not be misled: "Bad company corrupts good character." 1 Corinthians 15:33 NIV

When looking at various pictures of Klara Hitler, one sees a deeply saddened person who lost children to early death and was married to an abusive man. Alois sowed unfaithfulness, hardness, and brutality into his wife, and her pictures reflected this. His sin left a wide open door for destructive behavior, which not only affected his family but was used by Satan to shake the entire world.

Chapter 24

Nephilim Breeding Pattern

Psychopaths, both males and females, tend to choose immoral lifestyles. Dr. Hare, a psychologist and a leader in the field of psychopathy, shares perfectly the Nephilim breeding pattern of Genesis 6:1-2 with the Psychopathy's Strategy in Reproducing.

Dr. Hare relates that "sociobiology argues that psychopathy is not so much a psychiatric disorder as an expression of a particular genetically based reproductive strategy. Simply sociobiology asserts that one of our main roles in life is to reproduce, thereby passing our genes to the next generation. One reproductive strategy is to have so many children that some are bound to survive, even if they are neglected or abandoned. Psychopaths reproduce as often as possible and waste little energy in worrying about the welfare of their offspring. In this way, they propagate their genes with little or no personal investment. For male psychopaths, the most effective way to have lots of children is to mate with and quickly abandon a large number of women. Unless a psychopath is so attractive or charming that women actively pursue him, he can best accomplish his goal by deception, manipulation, cheating, and misrepresenting his status. Sociobiology believes that nature has provided us with various strategies for us to pass on our gene pool. One way is the 'cheating' strategy used by psychopaths. The behavior of female psychopaths also reflects a cheating strategy, one in which sexual relations are had with a large number of men and the welfare of the offspring is ignored." [219]

Sons of god did not seek to become a husband of one wife; this was not their goal. Sons of god were angels in rebellion to God's order and, as angels, they became visible from the vanishing point and would not be around long. They could disappear once they bred with a female, and she alone would be responsible for the offspring. Sound familiar?

> That the sons of God saw the daughters of men that they [were] fair; and they took them wives of **all** which **they chose**. Genesis 6:2 KJV

The word *wives* can make us think in terms of fidelity, but sons of God took as many wives (females) for sex as they wanted. Sons of God would breed, then leave and look for another woman as they chose to do so. Sex-filled worship with prostitution and orgies lured others to embrace their immoralities, even other nations like Israel. The term "orgy" used by the New Living Translation describes the atmosphere of their worship fest.

> Our worship of idols on the hills and our religious orgies on the mountains are a delusion. Only in the LORD our God will Israel ever find salvation. Jeremiah 3:23 NLT

Pagan ways promoted sex with strangers and unrestrained sexual activity. This is sex without morality or responsibility once again. This mode of sexual behavior did not originate from the Kingdom of God. Once established, immorality passed on to subsequence generations and set a Nephilim imprint. A Nephilim imprint on society arises when people accept Nephilim morality, as before the flood, in lifestyles, philosophies, or behaviors. Once anyone of these components finds acceptance contrary to the Word of God, a person acts on what he or she believes. In this manner, over a period of time, Nephilim ways become normalized, accepted, and thus imprinted on family lines and in a society. Nephilim strongholds become imbedded under the control of "spiritual forces of wickedness in heavenly places" (Ephesians 6:12 NIV).

For our struggle is not against flesh and blood, but against the rulers, against the powers, against the world forces of this darkness, against the spiritual forces of wickedness in the heavenly places. Ephesians 6:12 NIV

When God sent judgment against the sons of God of Genesis 6:4, chains stopped them from physically reproducing again, but nonetheless their genetics inbred into humans.

> And angels who had not kept their own original state, but had abandoned their own dwelling, he keeps in eternal chains under gloomy darkness, to the judgment of the great day. Jude 1:6 Darby Bible Translation

No wonder prostitution moves through Nephilim heritage; its origins come from them. Engaging in sex without commitment and leaving was normal. Abandonment of their babies was also a part of this heritage. What happened to unwanted babies produced as a result of prostitution? Perhaps their fate ended as human sacrifices to their gods or tossed out as trash. The nations that were a part of Hitler's heritage embraced these Nephilim lifestyles.

In the generations of Germany surrounding Alois Hitler's era, newborn babies did not warrant human status. If they were unwanted, they were thrown out to die or were killed. Historically, from this era the care of German infants was horrific as well, which could have easily left emotional scares. Sexual abuse was common place, even of their most vulnerable, children. [220] This mode of behavior and thinking was a Nephilim imprint that set the stage for genocide under Adolf Hitler.

Chapter 25

Nephilim/Psychopaths

At this point take another look at what has been learned about psychopaths with the Nephilim in mind. Psychopathic traits line up with Biblical descriptions of the Nephilim before and after the flood. Nephilim had no moral standards, restraint, or principles. Morality is defined as "conformity to the rules of right conduct; moral or virtuous conduct." [221] Sons of God rebelled, lied, deceived, and hid their true intent. Psychopaths ignore society's laws or twist them for their own purposes, just as sons of God ignored God's laws and pursued what they wanted no matter the effect on anyone else. Nephilim sought opportunities to rule over others. Goliath provides this example as he wanted to enslave all Israel under his tyrannical ego.

As Nephilim interbred and mingled with humans, "the intent of man's thoughts turned to evil continually as wickedness and violence filled the earth because of **them**" (Genesis 6:5, 13). This condition on earth did not come about until sons of God bred with daughters of men who created the Nephilim or psychopaths in subsequent generations.

> 11 Now the earth was corrupt in the sight of God, and the earth was filled with violence. 12 God looked on the earth, and behold, it was corrupt; for all flesh had corrupted their way upon the earth. 13 Then God said to Noah, "The end of all flesh has come before Me; **for the earth is filled with violence because of them;** and behold, I am about to destroy **them** with the earth. Genesis 6:11-13 NASB

Violence and terror became the way of life. The Hebrew word for violence, chamac, means "to do violence, wrong, cruelty, injustice, oppression, physical and ethical wrong," which scripturally refers to the presence of Nephilim. [222] These words easily describe the actions of psychopaths.

Males, females, young, old, single, married, poor, middle class, rich, all sizes, ages, shapes, skin color, nationalities, and different walks of life have psychopaths among them; for the most part, they cannot be detected by sight but by behavior. Nephilim inbred into humans to the point they also were not detected until their deeds exposed their presence. The same holds true for psychopaths. They're mixed in and nobody knows for sure how many truly exist. There are more male psychopaths than females and somewhere between "one to five percent of the general populations are thought to be psychopaths."[223][224] The U.S. population in 2012 can be estimated at 314 million. At three percent of this number, there could be over nine million psychopaths or more among us. The world population in this same year had an estimated seven billion people; three percent of this number makes 21 million psychopaths alive on earth, but again there could be many more.

People often describe these individuals as charming, manipulative, and without conscience. I have to make a comment on the use of the terms charming, manipulative, and without conscience. Charming defined as "using charm; exercising magic power."[225] Some may be thinking I am stretching here, but I am not the one describing these people. Exercising of magical power finds its source back to the sons of God who taught the use of magical power to their Nephilim descendants. [226] Magic powers were used to manipulate from the spirit realm to exercise control over others. Manipulative means "attempting to influence the behavior or emotions of others for one's own purposes." [227] Manipulative people use words to lure their victim in a trap. King

David describes this type of person.

> The words of their mouths are
> wicked and deceitful;. Even on
> their beds they plot evil; they
> committ themselves to a sinful
> course and do not reject what is
> wrong. Psalms 36:3a,4 NIV

Psychopaths do what they do because they want to. "Psychopaths commit an disproportionate amount of serious and violent crimes. Not all psychopaths are criminals, but of those who are, they display a predatory nature." [228] [229] The word predator is defined as "a person who habitually preys upon others; a hunter or a killer."[230] [231]

After the flood, the first man referenced as a "mighty man" (Hebrew word *gibbowr)* reveals the blending and continuation of Nephilim into mankind.[232] Who was Nimrod? He was a mighty hunter before the Lord. Nimrod was a violent, tyrannical ruler whose oppression and aggression was "in God's face." "Nimrod's tyranny became a proverb, hated both by God and man: for he did not cease to commit cruelty even in God's presence."[233]

He was a mighty hunter before the LORD; therefore it is said, "Like Nimrod a mighty hunter before the LORD." Genesis 10:9 NASB

Chapter 26

Nephilim Iniquity and Adolf Hitler

For reader ease I will add back the transference of iniquity noted previously in Adolf Hitler's life.

Immorality, sexual perversion, homosexuality, pornography, sexual depravity, multiple sex partners, pedophilia, incest, prostitution, merciless, despotism, arrogance, pride, tyrant, tyranny, addiction, deception, lying, violence, murder, mass murder, manipulation, spiritually immoral, self-exalted as god, false worship, occultism.

With this in mind, I believe all of these iniquities in one form or another can be traced to a Nephilim heritage. Not only did Nephilim propel paganism, immorality, perversion, corruption, deception, wickedness, idolatry, tyranny, violence, and murder, but addictions as well. Sons of god became addicted to sex. This point stands out as they took more and more wives (Genesis 6:2). The word *wife* in Genesis 6:2 is the "opposite of a male" and may refer to marriage but not necessarily. As a byproduct of multiple wives and sex partners, polygamy arose. [234] Polygamy's roots were of the sons of God or the Nephilim. Pornography also emerged in Nephilim cultures as numerous ancient artifacts illustrated sex acts and nudes.[235]

In these cultures, addictions to alcohol and drugs came as a result of religious events. One example of the Philistines "party spirit" occurred as they were "high" in spirits at a sacrifice to their god Dagon.

> 23Now the lords of the Philistines assembled to offer a great sacrifice to Dagon their god, and to rejoice, for they said, "Our god has given Samson our enemy into our hands." 25 It so happened when they were in **high spirits**, that they said, "Call for Samson, that he may amuse us." So they called for Samson from the prison, and he entertained them. And they

made him stand between the
pillars. Judges 16:25 NASB

Mystical activities such as witchcraft,
magic, charms, sorcery, astrological readings,
worship of the created sun, moon, and stars
are of Nephilim origins. Some believe Hitler
did not operate in occult practices, but I
certainly believe he did. Even the "god men"
philosophy Hitler embraced goes back to these
rebellious angels, and then further back to one
particular angel, Satan, who believed he also
was a god.

Chapter 27

Importance of Godly Husbands and Fathers

After Satan acquired access to mankind and their seed, the Nephilim way of life aimed at the destruction of marriage. A prize target would be to usurp the role of husband and father. If Nephilim immoral lifestyles became accepted by men, then men would walk away from their God given roles and responsibilities, just as the sons of God could do.

> But the Spirit explicitly says that in later times some will fall away from the faith, paying attention to deceitful spirits and doctrines of demons, 2by means of the hypocrisy of liars seared in their own conscience as with a branding iron, 3[men] who forbid marriage . . . 1 Timothy 4:1-3 NASB

In the last days people fall away from faith in the Word of God and follow deceitful spirits and doctrines of demons. What is a doctrine? A doctrine is an opinion or a principle.[236] In 1 Timothy 4:3, one of the doctrines forbidden was marriage. Forbidding marriage may also mean "withholding" of marriage.[237] If marriage is suppressed or withheld, then babies will be born without a covenantal relationship between their parents which opens opportunity for Nephilim imprints. Case in point, "According to the 2006-2010 National Survey of Family Growth (NSFG), 49.3 % of mothers between 15-44 years of age had non marital births. Cohabiting births rose from 12.4 % in 2002 to 21.9% in 2006-2010." [238]

Without righteous men accepting God's standards for morality, marriage, and fatherhood, more psychopaths come about. "Seventy percent of psychopaths are born to households lacking a father and thirty percent are born outside of marriage. Psychopaths are frequently children from broken households and those who never bonded with a father figure." [239] I noticed as I researched for this book that many psychopaths came from children of prostitutes. This duplicates the Nephilim breeding pattern. In these situations, a father or any positive father figure probably does not exist. Even if a positive father figure steps in to aid upbringing, a child can easily reject his input. So once again, when there is an evil seed, one uses others to get what he or she wants, even a father figure.

"A quote by Dr. Igor Galynker, associate chairman for the department of psychology at Beth Israel Medical Center in New York City "In a perfect environment, raised by well-meaning parents, you can still draw a psychopath." [240]

Think about the negative role model Alois Hitler provided his children as a father and husband. Both Alois Jr. and Adolf became like their father in many ways. A father figure for Alois had been Johann Georg Hiedler. Recall his occupation as a miller and their reputation as "cons and those who engaged in prostitution, gambling, excessive drinking and partying."[241] Alois certainly embraced an immoral lifestyle of this type, as did his generational line.

Numbers 14:18 states, "He will by no means clear the guilty, visiting the iniquity of the fathers on the children to the third and the fourth generations." By what we know of these men, and if we use Johann Georg Hiedler as the first generation, then Alois Hitler, next the third generation with Alois Jr. and Adolf Hitler, a trail of similar iniquity does exist even to the fourth generation. This clearly reveals Nephilim imprints pressed upon this family line. Some may think participation in some of the same choices as the Hitlers does not cause one to turn out like them. That would be good, but by repetition in the generations more opportunity arises for greater harm like what happened to the Hitler family line.

Chapter 28

Genealogy of Heaven or Earth

Genesis chapter one provides an overview of creation: the heavens, earth, and everything therein. Moses wrote Genesis chapter two with a different emphasis than the first chapter of Genesis. Genesis chapter one ends on day six, which happens to be the Biblical number for man.

> 1 Thus the heavens and the earth were completed, and all their hosts. 2 By the seventh day God completed His work which He had done, and He rested on the seventh day from all His work which He had done. 3 Then God blessed the seventh day and sanctified it, because in it He rested from all His work which God had created and made. Genesis 2:1-3 NASB

The work of God dealing with man spans to day seven of creation. A day in our understanding is a twenty-four hour period, but we also recognize it is a division of time. We do not know how long a "day" or this separation of time actually may be in Genesis chapter two.[242]

> But do not let this one fact escape your notice, beloved, that with the Lord one day is like a thousand years, and a thousand years like one day. 2 Peter 3:8 NASB

In Genesis 2:1, the work of day six was finished and by the seventh day, (the Biblical number for God), "He rested from all his work which God had created and made." His work of creation was done. Interestingly, "the number seven also indicates spiritual perfection (Genesis 2:3)." [243] Furthermore, on day seven when God's work is completed, the armies of heaven finally rest from war (Genesis 2:1-3).[244] We understand this by *tsaba,* the Hebrew word for host, which means "that which goes forth, army, war, warfare." [245] The armies of heaven cannot rest from warfare against Satan and his forces just yet. We are still in day six of creation. Just watch the news to understand our world fails greatly at perfection. God is taking us to day seven, but now in day six, war plays out for the souls of mankind on earth.

Next, in Genesis 2:4, Moses tells us about the generations of man.

> 4These are the generations of the heavens and of the earth when they were created, in the day that the LORD God made the earth and the heavens, Genesis 2:4 KJV

Towlĕdah, the Hebrew word for generations, references "an account of men and their descendants, which is also a genealogical list."[246] Moses wanted us to know there are generations of heaven and generations of earth, and that they are different from one another. A person will be among those of heaven or of the earth and those who perish with it (Luke 10:20).

"The man" Adam was created eternal until he broke the command of God and sinned. At that point, he died spiritually, but his body lived on a total of 930 years. This Hebrew word for lived, *chayay,* in Genesis 5:5 does means to "remain alive, which Adam did until his physical death." [247]

And all the days that Adam lived were nine hundred and thirty years: and he died. Genesis 5:5 KJV

Genesis chapter five lists the genealogy of Adam which began with his son Seth. Adam repented and was restored back to his relationship with God. Seth, like his dad, can be found listed in the genealogy of heaven. When Cain murdered his brother Abel, he left the presence of God. Cain became the first patriarch listed in the genealogy of earth. Moses does not list Cain or his lineage with Adam's descendants.

Chapter 29

Who's Your Daddy?

9 By this the love of God was
manifested in us that God has
sent His only begotten Son into
the world so that we might live
through Him. 10 In this is love,
not that we loved God, but that
He loved us and sent His Son *to
be* the propitiation for our sins. 1
John 4:9-10 NASB

All of us are born into Adam's sin and
have personally done deeds to our own shame
and condemnation. God, our Heavenly Father,
made a way for all mankind to be restored
back to His family and in His mercy. He sent a
second Adam, Jesus Christ, who did not fail
when Satan tempted him (Matthew 4:1-12).

For there is one God, and one
mediator also between God and
men, the man Christ Jesus . . .
1 Timothy 2:5 NASB

And there is salvation in no one
else; for there is no other name
under heaven that has been
given among men by which we
must be saved. Acts 4:12 NASB

We must first truly repent for our
sins, like Adam and Eve did, to be
restored to the genealogy of heaven. The
blood of the innocent was shed for the
guilty. Jesus, both God and man, born of a
virgin by the power of the Holy Spirit,
never sinned. He had to live without sin to
become the perfect sacrifice. Jesus bore
the penalty for the sins of all humanity
when He died on a cross. Buried and three
days later, by the power of God, His body
came back to life. He returned to heaven
and sits by the right hand of God, the
Father always interceding for us
(Matthew 1:18-25, I Peter 2:24, Acts
10:38-43).

8 But what does it say? "THE WORD IS NEAR YOU, IN YOUR MOUTH AND IN YOUR HEART"—that is, the word of faith which we are preaching, 9 that if you confess with your mouth Jesus as Lord, and believe in your heart that God raised Him from the dead, you will be saved; 10 for with the heart a person believes, resulting in righteousness, and with the mouth he confesses, resulting in salvation. Romans 10:8-10 NASB

If an individual has never asked Jesus to be his/her personal Lord and Savior, then what He did on the cross does not apply to them. Without Jesus, a person would pay the penalty for one's own sins, and the individual will be listed with the generations of the earth, separated from the Heavenly Father. Upon death, hell would be the sinner's punishment and final destination with the father of all sinners, Satan.

Jesus said, "In my Father's house there are many rooms and I will go and prepare a place for you (John 14:2)." If the reader has not repented of his/her sins, Satan will have successfully kept your soul for eternal punishment and away from a room in our Heavenly Father's house (Matthew 25:31-46).

If the reader would like to enter into a relationship with the Heavenly Father, it is time to pray.

> Heavenly Father, I recognize I am a sinner. Please forgive me for all my wrongdoing. I am sorry and I want Jesus to save me. Lord Jesus you bore all sin and the punishment I deserve on the cross. I ask you to make me clean. Come into my heart and be my Lord and Savior. I choose to simply believe your word. I thank you because I ask; you answer this prayer and take me out of the Kingdom of Darkness and place me into the Kingdom of Light.

If the reader has drifted away from the Lord and would like to repent and come back, pray the above prayer and mean it.

After all is said and done, eternity depends on the answer to one question: Who's your daddy? Two choices exist: the Heavenly Father, through faith in Jesus Christ, or Satan. May the reader choose correctly: it is a matter of eternal life or death.

The LORD rewarded me according to my righteousness; according to the cleanness of my hands hath he recompensed me 21 For I have kept the ways of the LORD, and have not wickedly departed from my God. Psalm 18:20-21

Source Notes

Article from FBI Law Enforcement Bulletin

1 Robert D. Hare and Matthew H. Logan, "Criminal Psychopathy: An Introduction for Police," in *The Psychology of Criminal Investigations: The Search for the Truth*, ed. Michel St-Yves and Michel Tanguay (Cowansville, QC: Editions Yvon Blais, 2009).

2 Hare and Logan, "Criminal Psychopathy: An Introduction for Police."

3. Paul J. Frick and Monica A. Marsee, "Psychopathy and Developmental Pathways to Antisocial Behavior in Youth," in *Handbook of Psychopathy*, ed. Christopher J. Patrick (New York, NY: Guilford Press, 2006), 353-374; and Donald R. Lynam, "Early Identification of Chronic Offenders: Who is the Fledgling Psychopath?" *Psychological Bulletin* 120, no. 2 (1996): 209-234.

4 Angus W. MacDonald III and William G. Iacono, "Toward an Integrated Perspective on the Etiology of Psychopathy," in *Handbook of Psychopathy*, ed. Christopher J. Patrick (New York, NY: Guilford Press, 2006), 375-385.

5 Dewey G. Cornell, Janet Warren, Gary Hawk, Ed Stafford, Guy Oram, and Denise Pine, "Psychopathy in Instrumental and Reactive Violent Offenders," *Journal of Consulting and Clinical Psychology* 64, no. 4 (August 1996): 783-790; J. Reid Meloy, *The Psychopathic Mind: Origins, Dynamics, and Treatment* (Northvale, NJ: Jason Aronson, 1988); and Michael Woodworth and Stephen Porter, "In Cold Blood: Characteristics of Criminal Homicides as a

[6] J. Reid Meloy and M.J. Meloy, "Autonomic Arousal in the Presence of Psychopathy: A Survey of Mental Health and Criminal Justice Professionals," *Journal of Threat Assessment* 2, no.2 (2002): 21-34.

[7] Meloy, *The Psychopathic Mind: Origins, Dynamics, and Treatment*; and Stephen Porter and Michael Woodworth, "Psychopathy and Aggression," in *Handbook of Psychopathy*, ed. Christopher J. Patrick (New York, NY: Guilford Press, 2006), 481-494.

[8] Mary Ellen O'Toole, "Psychopathy as a Behavior Classification System for Violent and Serial Crime Scenes," in *The Psychopath: Theory, Research, and Practice*, ed. Hugues Hervé and John C. Yuille (Mahwah, NJ: Lawrence Erlbaum and Associates, 2007), 301-325; and Woodworth and Porter, "In Cold Blood: Characteristics of Criminal Homicides as a Function of Psychopathy."

[9] Woodworth and Porter, "In Cold Blood: Characteristics of Criminal Homicides as a Function of Psychopathy."

[10] Paul Babiak, "When Psychopaths Go to Work," *Applied Psychology: An International Review* 44, no. 2 (1995):171-188; and Paul Babiak and Robert D. Hare, *Snakes in Suits: When Psychopaths Go to Work* (New York, NY: Harper/Collins, 2006).

[12] Grant T. Harris, Marnie E. Rice, Vernon L. Quinsey, Martin L. Lalumière, Douglas Boer, and Carol Lang, "A Multisite Comparison of Actuarial Risk Instruments for Sex Offenders," *Psychological Assessment* 15, no. 3 (2003): 413-425.

[13] Stephen Porter, Leanne ten Brinke, and Kevin Wilson, "Crime Profiles and Conditional Release Performance of Psychopathic and

Nonpsychopathic Sexual Offenders," *Legal and Criminological Psychology* 14, no. 1 (February 2009): 109-118.

14 Robert D. Hare, "Psychopaths and Their Nature: Implications for the Mental Health and Criminal Justice Systems," in *Psychopathy: Antisocial, Criminal, and Violent Behavior*, ed. Theodore Millon, Erik Simonsen, Morten Birket-Smith, and Roger D. Davis (New York, NY: Guilford Press, 1998), 188-212.

15 Helinä Häkkänen-Nyholm and Robert D. Hare, "Psychopathy, Homicide, and the Courts: Working the System," *Criminal Justice and Behavior* 36, no. 8 (2009): 761-777.

17 Porter, ten Brinke, and Wilson, "Crime Profiles and Conditional Release Performance of Psychopathic and Nonpsychopathic Sexual Offenders."

18 Meloy, The Psychopathic Mind: Origins, Dynamics, and Treatment.

19 Robert D. Hare, "Psychopathy, Affect, and Behavior," in *Psychopathy: Theory, Research, and Implications for Society,* ed. David J. Cooke, Adelle E. Forth, and Robert D. Hare (Dordrecht, The Netherlands: Kluwer, 1998), 105-137.

Source Notes

Origins of Psychopath

1 Psychopathy An Important Forensic Concept for the 21st Century." *FBI. N.p., n.d.* Web.<http://www.fbi.gov/stats-services/publications/law-enforcement-bulletin/july-2012/focus-on-psychopathy>. Apr. 29, 2013.

2. "Twin Study Finds Genetic Cause for Psychopathy." *Future Pundit.* http://www.sott.net/articles/show/147815-Twins-Study-Finds-Genetic-Cause-For-Psychopathy .June 23, 2012.

3 Psychopathy An Important Forensic Concept for the 21st Century." *FBI. N.p., n.d.* Web.<http://www.fbi.gov/stats-services/publications/law-enforcement-bulletin/july-2012/focus-on-psychopathy>. Apr. 29, 2013.

4. "Psychopathy Traits in Children Becoming Alarmingly Familiar to More Parents." *ABC News Radio* Thu, 03 Nov 2011 http://www.sott.net/articles/show/237326-Psychopathy-Traits-in-Children-Becoming-Alarmingly-Familiar-to-More-Parents. July 7, 2012.

5. Brains of Psychopaths are Different British Researchers find. Mark Henderson, *The Times*, August 3, 2009. http://www.sott.net/articles/show/190609-Brains-of-psychopaths-are-different-British-researchers-find. Jun 23, 2012.

6. "Psychopaths' Brains Wired to Seek Rewards, No Matter the Consequences. http://www.freerepublic.com/focus/f-chat/2470887/posts. April 19, 2013.

7. Meg Marquardt. "Psychopaths have brain structure abnormality." *Examiner.com.* http://www.freerepublic.com/focus/f-chat/2308247/posts. July 7, 2012.

8. "sin." *Collins English Dictionary - Complete & Unabridged 10th Edition.* HarperCollins Publishers. <Dictionary.com http://dictionary.reference.com/browse/sin>. Jul 5, 2012.

9. curse. Dictionary.com. *Collins English Dictionary - Complete & Unabridged 10th Edition.* HarperCollins Publishers. http://dictionary.reference.com/browse/curse. December 17, 2011.

10. Exodus 34:6-7, Exodus 20:5, also Jeremiah 32:18.

11. Blue Letter Bible. "Dictionary and Word Search for barak (Strong's 1288)". *Blue Letter Bible. 1996-2012.* < http:// www.blueletterbible.org/lang/lexicon/lexicon.cfm? Strongs=H1288&t=KJV >. Jul 17, 2012.

12. Human Genome Project Human Migration. How do genes tell the story of our ancient ancestor migration? http://www.ornl.gov/sci/techresources/Human_Genome/elsi/humanmigration.shtml. January 12, 2012.

13. Blue Letter Bible. "Dictionary and Word Search for "'son*" AND "H1121'" in the KJV". Blue Letter Bible. 1996-2012. < http:// www.blueletterbible.org/search/translationResults.cfm? Criteria=son%2A+H1121&t=KJV >. Jan 11, 2012.

14. "iniquity." *Dictionary.com Unabridged.* Random House, Inc. <Dictionary.com http://dictionary.reference.com/browse/iniquity >. Feb 2, 2012.

15. Blue Letter Bible. "Dictionary and Word Search for `avon (Strong's 5771)". Blue *Letter Bible. 1996-2012.* < http:// www.blueletterbible.org/lang/lexicon/lexicon.cf m? Strongs=H5771&t=KJV >. Jun 28, 2012.

16."visiting." Dictionary.com Unabridged. Random House, Inc. <Dictionary.com http://dictionary.reference.com/browse/visiting >. Jun. 30, 2012.

17."crafty." Dictionary.com Unabridged. Random House, Inc. <Dictionary.com http://dictionary.reference.com/browse/crafty>. Jul. 01, 2012.

18. Blue Letter Bible. "Dictionary and Word Search for Nowd (Strong's 5113)". *Blue Letter Bible.* 1996-2011. < http:// www.blueletterbible.org/lang/lexicon/lexicon.cf m? Strongs=H5113&t=KJV > Dec 22, 2011.

19. Klein, John, and Adam Spears. *Devils and demons and the return of the nephilim.* Fairfax: Xulon Press, 2005. P.82. May 7, 2012.

20. Blue Letter Bible. "Dictionary and Word Search for Chanowk (Strong's 2585)". *Blue Letter Bible. 1996-2011.* < http:// www.blueletterbible.org/lang/lexicon/lexicon.cf m? Strongs=H2585&t=NIV >. Dec 20, 2011.

21. Blue Letter Bible. "Dictionary and Word Search for `Iyrad (Strong's 5897)". *Blue Letter Bible. 1996-2011.* 22.< http:// www.blueletterbible.org/lang/lexicon/lexicon.cfm? Strongs=H5897&t=NIV >. Dec. 20, 2011.

22. Blue Letter Bible. "Dictionary and Word Search for Mĕchuwya'el (Strong's 4232)". *Blue Letter Bible. 1996-2011.* < http:// www.blueletterbible.org/lang/lexicon/lexicon.cfm? Strongs=H4232&t=NIV >. Dec 2, 2011.

23. Blue Letter Bible. "Dictionary and Word Search for *Mĕthuwsha'el (Strong's 4967)*". *Blue Letter Bible.* 1996-2011. < http:// www.blueletterbible.org/lang/lexicon/lexicon.cfm? Strongs=H4967&t=NIV >. Dec 20, 2011.

24. Blue Letter Bible. "Dictionary and Word Search for *Lemek (Strong's 3929)*". *Blue Letter Bible. 1996-2011.* < http:// www.blueletterbible.org/lang/lexicon/lexicon.cfm? Strongs=H3929&t=KJV >. Dec 22, 2011.

25. Blue Letter Bible. "Dictionary and Word Search for *'Enowsh (Strong's 583)*". *Blue Letter Bible. 1996-2011.* < http:// www.blueletterbible.org/lang/lexicon/lexicon.cfm? Strongs=H583&t=KJV >. Dec 30, 2011.

26. Blue Letter Bible. "Dictionary and Word Search for *Qeynan (Strong's 7018)*". *Blue Letter Bible. 1996-2011.* < http:// www.blueletterbible.org/lang/lexicon/lexicon.cfm? Strongs=H7018&t=KJV >. Dec 30, 2011.

27. Blue Letter Bible. "Dictionary and Word Search for *Mahalal'el (Strong's 4111)*". Blue Letter Bible. 1996-2011. < http:// www.blueletterbible.org/lang/lexicon/lexicon.cfm? Strongs=H4111&t=KJV >.

28. Blue Letter Bible. "Dictionary and Word Search for *Yered (Strong's 3382)*". Blue Letter Bible. 1996-2011. < http://www.blueletterbible.org/lang/lexicon/lexicon.cf m? Strongs=H3382&t=KJV >. Dec 30, 2011.

29. Blue Letter Bible. "Dictionary and Word Search for *Chanowk (Strong's 2585)*". Blue Letter Bible. 1996-2011. < *http:// www.blueletterbible.org/lang/lexicon/lexicon.cf m? Strongs=H2585&t=KJV* >. Dec 30, 2011.

30. Blue Letter Bible. "Dictionary and Word Search for *Lemek (Strong's 3929)*". Blue Letter Bible. 1996-2011. < *http:// www.blueletterbible.org/lang/lexicon/lexicon.cf m? Strongs=H3929&t=KJV* >. Dec 30, 2011.

31. Blue Letter Bible. "Dictionary and Word Search for *Noach (Strong's 5146)*". Blue Letter Bible. 1996-2011. < *http:// www.blueletterbible.org/lang/lexicon/lexicon.cf m? Strongs=H5146&t=KJV* >. Dec 30, 2011.

32. Langer, Walter C. *The Mind of Adolf Hitler; the Secret Wartime Report*. New York: Basic, 1972. Print.

33."Analysis of Hitler's Personality." Analysis of Hitler's Personality. N.p., n.d. http://www.lawschool.cornell.edu/library/what wehave/specialcollections/donovan/hitler/. Mar 25, 2013.

34. Langer, Walter C. *The Mind of Adolf Hitler; the Secret Wartime Report*. New York: Basic, 1972. P.16. Print.

35. Ibid., 269.

36. Ibid., 140

37. Langer, Walter C. *The Mind of Adolf Hitler; the Secret Wartime Report.* New York: Basic, 1972. P. 140. Print.

38."Ancestry of Adolf Hitler." About.com N.p.,n.d.http://history1900s.about.com/od/hitleradolf/a /hitlerancestry.htm. Mar 26, 2013.

39. Langer, Walter C. The Mind of Adolf Hitler; the Secret Wartime Report. New York: Basic, 1972. p.111, 265.

40. Ibid.

41. Hitler's Jewish Ancestors. Lloyd Thomas. http://lloydthomas.org/1-IsraelTimeLine/7-1930-1999/hitler.html. . Feb 5, 2012.

42. Langer, Walter C. p 111-113.

43. Hitler's Jewish Ancestors. Lloyd Thomas. *http://lloydthomas.org/1-IsraelTimeLine/7-1930-1999/hitler.html.* Feb 5, 2012.

44. Find a Grave. Alois Hitler. Kit and Morgan Benson.http://www.findagrave.com/cgi-bin/fg.cgi?page=gr&GRid=11646. June 10, 2012.

45. Hitler's Jewish Ancestors. Lloyd Thomas. *http://lloydthomas.org/1-IsraelTimeLine/7-1930-1999/hitler.html.* Feb 5, 2012.

46. Ibid.

47. Ibid.

48. Langer, Walter C. *The Mind of Adolf Hitler; the Secret Wartime Report.* New York: Basic, 1972. P.112, 113, 265. Print.

49. Ibid., 111.

50."Hitler and Family." Eureka Encypedia, <http://www.eurekaencyclopedia.com/index.php/Cat egory:Hitler_and_Family>. Mar 27, 2013.

51. Langer, Walter C. *The Mi nd of Adolf Hitler; the Secret Wartime Report.* New York: Basic, 1972. P. 114.

52. J Hitler's Jewish Ancestors. Lloyd Thomas. *http://lloydthomas.org/1-IsraelTimeLine/7-1930-1999/hitler.html.* Jan 6, 2012.

53. Ibid

54. Ibid.

55. Langer, Walter C. *The Mind of Adolf Hitler; the Secret Wartime Report.* New York: Basic, 1972. P., 114.

56. Ibid.

57. Ibid., 114-117.

58. Ibid.

59. Ibid

60. Ibid

61. Langer, Walter C. *The Mind of Adolf Hitler; the Secret Wartime Report.* New York: Basic, 1972. P., 114.

62. Ibid., 117.

63. Ibid., 115.

64. Ibid

65. Ibid.

66. Ibid.

67. Ibid. 256.

68. Ibid

69. Ibid., 117

70. Ibid., 61

71. Ibid., 255.

72. Langer, Walter C. *The Mind of Adolf Hitler; the Secret Wartime Report.* New York: Basic, 1972. P.,159.

73. Ibid

74. Ibid., 160.

75. Ibid.

76. Ibid., 160, 161.

77. Ibid., 118

78. Ibid., 118, 119

79. Ibid

80. Ibid.

81. Ibid., 129-131

82. Ibid.

83. Ibid.

84. "The Hidden Hitler." Lothar Machtan. http://www.angelfire.com/linux/thehiddenhitler/. Apr 2, 2013.

85. Ibid

86. Ibid.

87. Ibid., 185,195.

88. Ibid. 193-194.

89. Ibid., 256-257.

90. Ibid

91. Ibid., 191-192

92. Ibid. 192.

93. Ibid., 188,189, 191.

94. Ibid., 149, 188,189, 191.

95. Ibid., 100-101

96. Ibid

97. Ibid.

98. Ibid

99. Ibid.101.

100. Ibid. 127.

101. Langer, Walter C. *The Mind of Adolf Hitler; the Secret Wartime Report.* New York: Basic, 1972. P.195.

102. Ibid., 103.

103. Ibid., 265-266

104. Ibid., 83-86.

105. Ibid., 250.

106. Rosenbaum, Ron. *Explaining Hitler: The Search for the Origins of His Evil*. New York: Random House, 1998. P. 104. Print.

107. Langer, Walter C. *The Mind of Adolf Hitler; the Secret Wartime Report*. New York: Basic, 1972. .34-35, 37, 60.

108. "occult." *Dictionary.com Unabridged*. Random House, Inc. <Dictionary.com http://dictionary.reference.com/browse/occult>. Apr 18, 2012.

109. Langer, Walter C. *The Mind of Adolf Hitler; the Secret Wartime Report*. New York: Basic, 1972. P. 111.

110. Ibid.

111. Ibid.

112. *72 Interesting Facts about Adolf Hitler*. N.p., n.d. Web. <http://facts.randomhistory.com/hitler-facts.html>. Apr 6, 2013.

113. Adolf Hitler's Family Tree. http://thegenealogycorner.wordpress.com/2012/01/22/adolf-hitlers-family-tree/. Feb 7, 2012.

114. Nazis 'gassed Hitler's relative. 'http://news.bbc.co.uk/2/hi/europe/4187823.stm. Feb 6, 2012

115. Adolf Hitler's Family Tree. http://thegenealogycorner.wordpress.com/2012/01/22/adolf-hitlers-family-tree/. Feb 7, 2012.

116. Ibid

117.Johann-Georg-Hiedler http://www.factbites.com/topics/Johann-Georg-Hiedler. Feb 6, 2012.

118. Hitler's Jewish Ancestors. Lloyd Thomas. http://lloydthomas.org/1-IsraelTimeLine/7-1930-1999/hitler.html. Apr 6, 2013.

119. Ibid.

120. German Village. A Brief Description of a Southern German Village in the Past Centuries. Dieter, Joos. http://geisheimer.org/info/germ/village.htm. Apr 15, 2013.

121. Langer, Walter C. *The Mind of Adolf Hitler; the Secret Wartime Report*. New York: Basic, 1972. P. 111.

122. Ibid.

123. Ibid, 118-119.

124. Ibid.

125. Ibid.

126. Langer, Walter C. *The Mind of Adolf Hitler; the Secret Wartime Report*. New York: Basic, 1972. P. 118-119.

127. Ibid.

128. Ibid., 121.

129. Langer, Walter C. The Mind of Adolf Hitler; the Secret Wartime Report. New York: Basic, 1972. 160.

130. Doctor Erwin Jekelius. http://www.geni.com/people/Erwin-Jekelius/6000000010780561949. Apr 8, 2013.

131.   Heinrich   "Heinz"   Hitler.
http://www.findagrave.com/cgi-
bin/fg.cgi?page=gr&GRid=12465553 Apr 8, 2012.

132. Langer, Walter C. *The Mind of Adolf
Hitler; the Secret Wartime Report.* New York: Basic,
1972. P. 120

133. Ibid.

134. Ibid.

135. Joachimsthaler, Anton. *Hitlers Liste: Ein
Dokument Personlicher Beziehungen.* Herbig. p. 271.
Feb 9, 2012.

136. "DNA tests reveal Hitler's Jewish and
African roots." Haaretz.com.. Haaretz Services.
http://www.haaretz.com/jewish-world/dna-tests-
reveal-hitler-s-jewish-and-african-roots-1.309938. Feb
13, 2012.

137. Ibid.

138. Ibid.

139. "DNA tests reveal Hitler's Jewish and
African roots." Haaretz.com.. *Haaretz Services.*
http://www.haaretz.com/jewish-world/dna-tests-
reveal-hitler-s-jewish-and-african-roots-1.309938. Feb
11. 2012.

140. "DNA Tests Reveal Hitler Was
Descended from the Jews and Africans He Hated."
Mail   Online.   N.p.,   n.d.   Web.
<http://www.dailymail.co.uk/news/article-
1305414>.Feb 13, 2012.

141. African People & Culture, Tribes &
People   Groups   Berber.
http://www.africaguide.com/culture/tribes/berber.htm.
Feb 11, 2012.

142. Ibid.

143. "Dancing from Genesis. Sons of Canaanite Posidon of Atlit were Ancestors of Berber and Tuareg Tribes of Northwest Africa Showing Atlantean Connection through Usage of Atl Etymology for Water. Jams I. Niehuis. " *http://dancingfromgenesis.wordpress.com/200 7/10/26/sons-of-canaanite-posidon-of-atlit-were-ancestors-of-berber-and-tuareg-tribes-of-northwest-africa-showing-atlantean-connection-through-usage-of-atl-etymology-for-water/.* Feb 16, 2012

144. "Ashkenazic and Sephardic Jews " Judism 101. http://www.jewfaq.org/ashkseph.htm. Feb 13, 2012

145. Weiner, Rebecca. "Sephardim." *http://www.jewishvirtuallibrary.org/jsource/Judaism/Sephardim.html.* Apr 9, 2013.

146. Sephardic Gen Resources. *Sephardicgen.com* *http://www.sephardicgen.com/seph_who.htm.* Feb 22, 2012.

147. The Table of Nations: Genesis Chapters 10-11. Lambert Dolphin . *http://www.ldolphin.org/ntable.html.* Feb 16, 2012.

148. "Ashkenazic and Sephardic Jews." *Judanism 101.* *http://www.jewfaq.org/ashkseph.htm.* Feb 18, 2012.

149. Ibid.

150. Ibid.

151. "polygamy." *Dictionary.com Unabridged.* Random House, Inc. *<Dictionary.com http://dictionary.reference.com/browse/polygamy>.* Feb 19, 2012.

152. "Berber, Filala of Morocco".Joshua Project. *http://www.joshuaproject.net/people-profile.php?rop3=101273&rog3=MO.* Feb 19, 2012

153. "The Big Question What's the History of Polygamy and How Serious a Problem is it in Africa?" Independent.co.uk/news/world/Africa. http://www.independent.co.uk/news/world/africa/the-big-question-whats-the-history-of-polygamy-and-how-serious-a-problem-is-it-in-africa-1858858.html. Feb 18, 2012.

154. Joachim C.Fest, *Hitler.* Verlagg Ulstein. (1973). print.

155. "religion." *Collins English Dictionary - Complete & Unabridged 10th Edition.* HarperCollins Publishers. <Dictionary.com 19, 2012.*http://dictionary.reference.com/browse/religion>. Feb 19, 2012.*

156. "Polygamy/Confucianism." *New World Encyclopedia.* *http://www.newworldencyclopedia.org/entry/Polygamy #Confucianism.* Feb 19, 2012.

157. Jay Sand. "Jews of Africa." http://www.mindspring.com/~jaypsand/morocco2.htm. Apr 10, 2013.

158. Ibid.

159. Norman L. Greene. Morocco News Board. http://www.moroccoboard.com/news/5012-journey-into-moroccan-history-a-visit-to-the-jews-of-morocco-exhibition-at-nys-center-for-jewish-history. Feb 20, 2012

160.Berbers. http://www.encyclopedia.com/topic/Berbers.as px. Feb 23, 2012..

161. Ibid.

162. Berbers Jewish Virtual Library *http://www.jewishvirtuallibrary.org/jsource/ju daica/ejud_0002_0003_002599.html.* Feb 23, 2012.

163. David Hart. *Tribe and Society in Rural* Marocco. Routledge (October 1, 2000). Print. p. 37-39.

164. Ibid.

165. Ibid.

166. "The History of Israel – Sons of Noah."http://www.israel-a-history-of.com/sons-of-noah.html#<u>Ham - son of Noah</u>. Feb 27, 2012.

167. Ibid.

168. Legacy of the Ancient Egyptian. http://legacyoftheancientegyptians.weebly.com /religion.html. Apr 30, 2012.

169. Ibid.

170. Ibid.

171. "The History of Israel – Sons of Noah."http://www.israel-a-history-of.com/sons-of-noah.html#<u>Ham - son of Noah</u>. Feb 27, 2012.

172. Ibid.

173. Legacy of the Ancient Egyptian. http://legacyoftheancientegyptians.weebly.com /religion.html. Apr 30, 2012.

174. "Ancient Egyptian Beliefs, Customs, Traditions, Superstitions Regarding the Afterlife." http://history.factoidz.com/ancient-egyptian-beliefs-traditions-superstitions-regarding-the-afterlife/. Feb 24, 2012.

175. Caroline Seawright. "Ancient Egyptian Sexuality." *http://www.touregypt.net/featurestories/sexuality.htm . February 25, 2012.*

176. Ibid.

177. Ibid.

178. Ibid.

179. Ibid.

180. Ibid.

181. Families-Children-Egyptian-Marriage *http://unusualhistoricals.blogspot.com/2008/05/familie s-children-egyptian-marriage.html*. Feb 26, 2012.

182. Ibid.

183. "The History of Israel – Sons of Noah." http://www.israel-a-history-of.com/sons-of-noah.html#<u>Ham - son of Noah</u>. Feb 23, 2012.

184. Canaanite Religion New World Encyclopedia. http://www.newworldencyclopedia.org/entry/Canaanit e_Religion. Apr 12, 2013.

185. Ibid.

186. A. D. Godley. *Herodotus, with an English translation*. Cambridge. Harvard University Press. 1920.

187. Richard T. Ritenbaugh. "Who were the Philistines?" http://www.cgg.org/index.cfm/fuseaction/Libra ry.sr/CT/PW/k/1183/Who-Were-Philistines.htm#ixzz1gSjjfRrS. Apr 13, 2013.

188. Ibid.

189. "Ancient Ashkelton." *National Geographic* .http://ngm.nationalgeographic.com/print/feat ures/world/asia/israel/ashkelon-text. Mar 5, 2012.

190. Blue Letter Bible. "Dictionary and Word Search for `Anaqiy (Strong's 6062)*". *Blue Letter Bible. 1996-2012.* < http:// www.blueletterbible.org/lang/lexicon/lexicon.cf m? *Strongs=H6062&t=KJV >.* Feb 27, 2012.

191. Blue Letter Bible. "Dictionary and Word Search for *Chebrown (Strong's 2275)*". *Blue Letter Bible. 1996-2012.* < http:// www.blueletterbible.org/lang/lexicon/lexicon.cf m?*Strongs=H2275&t=NASB >.* Mar 5, 2012.

192. Blue Letter Bible. "Dictionary and Word Search for cheber (Strong's 2267)". *Blue Letter Bible. 1996-2012.* < http:// www.blueletterbible.org/lang/lexicon/Lexicon.c fm?
Strongs=H2267&t=KJV >. Feb 28, 2012.

193. Blue Letter Bible. "Dictionary and Word Search for 'Arba` (Strong's 704)". *Blue Letter Bible. 1996-2012.* < http:// www.blueletterbible.org/lang/lexicon/lexicon.cf m?
Strongs=H704&t=KJV >. Feb 28, 2012.

194. "dismayed." *Dictionary.com Unabridged.* Random House, Inc.. *<Dictionary.com http://dictionary.reference.com/browse/dismayed>.* Feb 28, 2012.

195. V. Bryan. Living with the Nephilim the Seed of Destruction. V Ly Publishing, Print. 2013..

196. Ibid.

197. Blue Letter Bible. "Dictionary and Word Search for gibbowr (Strong's 1368)". *Blue Letter Bible. 1996-2011.* < *http://* www.blueletterbible.org/lang/lexicon/lexicon.cfm? Strongs=H1368&t=KJV >. Oct 4, 2011.

198. Blue Letter Bible. "Dictionary and Word Search for `owlam (Strong's 5769)*". *Blue Letter Bible. 1996-2011.* < http:// www.blueletterbible.org/lang/lexicon/lexicon.cfm? Strongs=H5769&t=KJV >. Oct 4, 2011.

199. Blue Letter Bible. "Dictionary and Word Search for `alam (Strong's 5956)". *Blue Letter Bible. 1996-2011.* < http:// www.blueletterbible.org/lang/lexicon/Lexicon.cfm? Strongs=H5956&t=KJV >. Oct 5, 2011.

200. "dissemble." Dictionary.com Unabridged. Random House, Inc. *<Dictionary.com http://dictionary.reference.com/browse/dissemble>.*May 8, 2011.

201. "feller." *Roget's 21st Century Thesaurus, Third Edition.* Philip Lief Group 2009. <Thesaurus.com http://thesaurus.com/browse/feller>. Oct 29, 2010.

202. Blue Letter Bible. "Dictionary and Word Search for 'giant* H5303' in the KJV". Blue Letter Bible. 1996-2010. < http://. www.blueletterbible.org/search/translationResults.cf m?

Strongs=H5303&Criteria=giant%2A&t=KJV
>. Oct 29, 2010.

203. "feller." *Roget's 21st Century Thesaurus, Third Edition*. Philip Lief Group 2009. 29 Oct. 2010. <Thesaurus.com http://thesaurus.com/browse/feller>.

204. Blue Letter Bible. "Dictionary and Word Search for *shem (Strong's 8034)*". *Blue Letter Bible. 1996-2011. < http:// www.blueletterbible.org/lang/lexicon/lexicon.cf m?*
Strongs=H8034&t=KJV >. Oct 5, 2010.

205. "bully." Dictionary.com Unabridged. Random House, Inc. <Dictionary.com http://dictionary.reference.com/browse/bully>. Oct 29, 2010.

206. "tyrant." Dictionary.com Unabridged. Random House, Inc. *<Dictionary.com* http://dictionary.reference.com/browse/tyrant>
.

207. "tyrant." *Online Etymology Dictionary*. Douglas Harper, Historian. *<Dictionary.com* http://dictionary.reference.com/browse/tyrant>
. Oct 4, 2011.

208. Ibid.

209. Adam Spears and John Klein. *Devils and demons and the return of the nephilim*. Fairfax: Xulon Press, 2005. p. 94.

210. "abortion." Dictionary.com Unabridged. Random House, Inc. <Dictionary.com. http://dictionary.reference.com/browse/abortion>. Mar 8, 2011

211. V. Bryan. Living with the Nephilim the Seed of Destruction. V Ly Publishing. 2013.

212. Twin Study Finds Genetic Cause for Psychopathy. *Future Pundit. http://www.sott.net/articles/show/147815.* Jun 23, 2012.

213. Jeffrey H. Schwarts and Ian Tattersall.
"Hominids and Hybrids: The place of Neanderthals in Human Evolution." http://www.pnas.org/content/96/13/7117.long. Apr 13, 2013.
214. Ibid

215. Dennis O'Neil. "Neanerthals." http://anthro.palomar.edu/homo2/mod_homo_2.htm. Mar 8, 2012.

216. K. Kris Hirst. "Human Migration." *http://archaeology.about.com/od/stoneage/ss/tishkoff_2 .htm.* Mar 8, 2012.

217. Blue Letter Bible. "Dictionary and Word Search for dabaq (Strong's 1692)". *Blue Letter Bible. 1996-2012.* < *http:// www.blueletterbible.org/lang/lexicon/lexicon.cfm? Strongs=H1692&t=KJV* >. Mar 31, 2012.

218. "Ashamed." Dictionary.com Unabridged. Random House, Inc. *<Dictionary.com http://dictionary.reference.com/browse/Ashamed>.* Apr 3, 2012.

219. Without Conscience The Disturbing World of The Psychopaths Among Us. New York, NY: Simon & Schuster Inc., 1993. P.166, 167.

220. Lloyd deMause. *The Origins of War.* "The Origins of War in Child Abuse" *http://www.psychohistory.com/originsofwar/06 _childhoodOrigins.html.* Jan 23, 2012.

221. "morality." Collins English Dictionary - Complete & Unabridged 10th Edition. HarperCollins Publishers. <Dictionary.com http://dictionary.reference.com/browse/moralit y>. Jul 25, 2012.

222. Blue Letter Bible. "Dictionary and Word Search for *chamac (Strong's 2555)*". *Blue Letter Bible. 1996-2012. < http:// www.blueletterbible.org/lang/lexicon/lexicon.cf m? Strongs=H2555&t=KJV >.* Jul 9, 2012.

223. Psychopathy An Important Forensic Concept for the 21st Century." FBI. N.p., n.d. Web. <http://www.fbi.gov/stats-services/publications/law-enforcement-bulletin/july-2012/focus-on-psychopathy>. Apr 21, 2013.

224. Hunter Darden. Personality Disorder, Causes of Sociopathic Behavior. *ehow.com http://www.ehow.com/about_5125823_causes-sociopathic-behavior.html.* Apr 29, 2013.

225. "charming." Dictionary.com Unabridged. Random House, Inc. 22 Apr. 2013. *<Dictionary.com http://dictionary.reference.com/browse/charmi ng>.* Apr.22, 2013.

226. V. Bryan. Living with the Nephilim the Seed of Destruction. V Ly Publishing, Print. 2013.

227. "manipulative." Dictionary.com Unabridged. Random House, Inc. *<Dictionary.com .http://dictionary.reference.com/browse/manipulative>* . Apr.22, 2013.

228. Psychopathy An Important Forensic Concept for the 21st Century." FBI. N.p., n.d. Web. <http://www.fbi.gov/stats-services/publications/law-enforcement-bulletin/july-2012/focus-on-psychopathy>. Apr 29, 2013.

229. Dr. Robert Hare, "FBI — Focus on Psychopathy." *FBI — Homepage*. N.p., n.d. Web.. <http://www.fbi.gov/stats-services/publications/law-enforcement-bulletin/july-2012/focus-on-psychopathy>. Apr 22, 2013.

230. "predator - Synonyms and More from the Free Merriam-Webster Dictionary." *Dictionary and Thesaurus - Merriam-Webster Online*. N.p., n.d. Web. 22 Apr. 2013. <http://www.merriam-webster.com/thesaurus/predator?show=0&t=1366663009>. Apr 22, 2013.

231. "predator." *Thesaurus.com*. N.p., Web. 22 Apr. 2013. <http://thesaurus.com/browse/predator?__utma=1.157 5534208. Apr 22, 2013.

232. Blue Letter Bible. "Dictionary and Word Search for gibbowr (Strong's 1368)". Blue Letter Bible. 1996-2013. < http:// www.blueletterbible.org/lang/lexicon/lexicon.cfm? Strongs=H1368&t=NIV > Apr 22, 2013.

233. "Genesis 10:9 He was a mighty hunter before the LORD; that is why it is said, "Like Nimrod, a mighty hunter before the LORD."." Online Parallel Bible: Weaving God's Word into the Web. N.p., n.d. Web. <http://bible.cc/genesis/10-9.htm>. Apr 23, 2013.

234. Blue Letter Bible. "Dictionary and Word Search for *'ishshah (Strong's 802)*". Blue Letter Bible. 1996-2012. < http://www.blueletterbible.org/lang/lexicon/lexicon.cfm?
Strongs=H802&t=NASB >. Feb 29, 2012.

235. Caroline Seawright. "Ancient Egyptian Sexuality." http://www.touregypt.net/featurestories/sexuality.htm. February 25, 2012.

236. Blue Letter Bible. "Dictionary and Word Search for *didaskalia (Strong's 1319)*". *Blue Letter Bible. 1996-2013.* < http://www.blueletterbible.org/lang/lexicon/lexicon.cfm?
Strongs=G1319&t=KJV >. Apr 17, 2013.

237. Blue Letter Bible. "Dictionary and Word Search for kōlyō (Strong's 2967)". Blue Letter Bible. 1996-2013. < http://www.blueletterbible.org/lang/lexicon/lexicon.cfm? Strongs=G2967&t=KJV >Jun 4, 2013.

238. Centers for Disease Control and Prevention. National Vital Statistics System. http://www.cdc.gov/nchs/data/databriefs/db18.pdf. Apr 15, 2013.

239. Ms. O. Rene McQuick. Antisocial-Personality-Disorder-Nature-or-Nurture?. *http://www.docstoc.com/docs/976127/Antisocial-Personality-Disorder-Nature-or-Nurture.* Apr 17, 2013

240. "Psychopathy Traits in Children Becoming Alarmingly Familiar to More Parents." ABC News Radio Thu, 03 Nov 2011 http://www.sott.net/articles/show/237326-Psychopathy-Traits-in-Children-Becoming-Alarmingly-Familiar-to-More-Parents. July 7, 2012.

241. Joos Dieter, German Village. A Brief Description of a Southern German Village in the Past Centuries. *http://geisheimer.org/info/germ/village.htm.* Apr 15, 2013.

242. Blue Letter Bible. "Dictionary and Word Search for *yowm (Strong's 3117)*". *Blue Letter Bible. 1996-2012.* < *http:// www.blueletterbible.org/lang/lexicon/lexicon.cfm? Strongs=H3117&t=KJV >.* Apr 13, 2012.

243. E. W. Bullinger. "The Meaning of Numbers in the Bible." *http://www.biblestudy.org/bibleref/meaning-of-numbers-in-bible/7.html.* Mar 26, 2012

244. Ibid.

245. Blue Letter Bible. "Dictionary and Word Search for *tsaba' (Strong's 6635)*". *Blue Letter Bible. 1996-2012.* < *http:// www.blueletterbible.org/lang/lexicon/lexicon.cfm? Strongs=H6635&t=KJV >.* Mar 26, 2012.

246. Blue Letter Bible. "Dictionary and Word Search for *towlĕdah (Strong's 8435)*". *Blue Letter Bible.*

247. Blue Letter Bible. "Dictionary and Word Search for *Strong's 2425)*". *Blue Letter Bible. 1996-2012.* < *http:// www.blueletterbible.org/lang/lexicon/lexicon.cfm? Strongs=H2425&t=KJV >.* Apr 1, 2012.

Sources

Adams, Jean, "Families-Children-Egyptian-Marriage."
http://unusualhistoricals.blogspot.com/2008/0
5/families-children-egyptian-marriage.html.

"Adolf Hitler's Family Tree." The Genealogy Corner.
http://thegenealogycorner.wordpress.com/201
2/01/22/adolf-hitlers-family-tree/

"African People & Culture, Tribes & People Groups Berber." *AfricianGuide.com*
http://www.africaguide.com/culture/tribes/be
rber.htm.

"Analysis of Hitler's Personality." *Cornell University Law Library.*
http://www.lawschool.cornell.edu/library.

"Ancestry of Adolf Hitler." About.com 20th Century History.
http://history1900s.about.com/od/hitleradolf/
a/hitlerancestry.htm.

"Ancient Egyptian Beliefs, Customs, Traditions, Superstitions Regarding the Afterlife." *History Factoidz.com.*
http://history.factoidz.com/ancient-egyptian-
beliefs-traditions-superstitions-regarding-
theafterlife/http://history.factoidz.com/ancien
t-egyptian-beliefs-traditions-superstitions-
regarding-the-afterlife/.

Ashkenazic and Sephardic Jews. *Judism 101.* http://www.jewfaq.org/ashkseph.htm.

"Berbers" *Jewish Virtual Library* - http://www.jewishvirtuallibrary.org/jsource/j udaica/ejud_0002_0003_0_02599.html.

"Biblos.com: Search, Read, Study the Bible in Many Languages." *Biblos.com: Search, Read, Study the Bible in Many Languages.* N.p., n.d. Web. <http://www.biblos.com/>.

"Blue Letter Bible-Dictionaries." *Blue Letter Bible - Dictionaries.* N.p., n.d. Web. 18 Sept. 2012. <http://cf.blueletterbible.org/Search/Dictiona ry/viewTopic.cfm?type=GetTopic>.

Bryan. V. *Living with the Nephilim the Seed of Destruction.* V Ly Publishing, 2013.

Canaanite Religion. New World Encyclopedia. http://www.newworldencyclopedia.org/entry/ Canaanite_Religion.

Centers for Disease Control and Prevention. National Vital Statistics System. http://www.cdc.gov/nchs/data/databriefs/db18 .pdf.

Collins English Dictionary - Complete & Unabridged 10th Edition. HarperCollins Publishers. 05 Jul. 2012. <Dictionary.com http://dictionary.reference.com/browse/sin>.

DeMause, Lloyd. "The Origins of War " *The Origins of War in Child Abuse*, http://www.psychohistory.com/originsofwar/0 6_childhoodOrigins.html.

"DNA Tests Reveal Hitler's Jewish and African roots." *Haaretz Digital Editions. Jewish World.* http://www.haaretz.com/jewish-world/dna-tests-reveal-hitler-s-jewish-and-african-roots-1.309938.

"DNA Tests Reveal 'Hitler Was Descended from the Jews and Africans He Hated'" *Mail Online.* N.p., n.d. Web. <http://www.dailymail.co.uk/news/article-1305414>.

Dolphin, Lambert. "The Table of Nations: Genesis Chapters 10-11." http://www.ldolphin.org/ntable.html.

Enhanced Strong's Lexicon. Logos Research Systems, Inc.

Fest, Joachim C. Verlagg Ulstein. *Hitler.* (1973).

"Genetic Origins of Antisocial Behaviour," *Twin Study. Enpsychopedia RSS.* N.p., n.d.

Gore, Rick. "Ancient Ashkelton." *National Geographic.* http://ngm.nationalgeographic.com/print/feat ures/world/asia/israel/ashkelon-text.

Greene, Norman L. *Morocco News Board.* http://www.moroccoboard.com/news/5012-journey-into-moroccan-history-a-visit-to-the-jews-of-morocco-exhibition-at-nys-center-for-jewish-history

Hare, Robert Dr. *Without Conscience The Disturbing World of The Psychopaths Among Us.* New York, NY: Simon & Schuster Inc.

Hart, David. Tribe and Society in Rural Marocco. Routledge (October 1, 2000). Print.

Heinrich "Heinz" Hitler. http://www.findagrave.com/cgi-bin/fg.cgi?page=gr&GRid=12465553.

Henderson, Mark. "Brains of Psychopaths are Different British Researchers find." The Times, August 3, 2009. http://www.sott.net/articles/show/190609-Brains-of-psychopaths-are-different-British-researchers-find

Herodotus, with an English translation. A. D. Godley. Cambridge. Harvard University Press. 1920.

Hirst, K. Kris. "Human Migration." . http://archaeology.about.com/od/stoneage/ss/t ishkoff_2.htm

Hitler's Jewish Ancestors. Lloyd Thomas. http://lloydthomas.org/1-IsraelTimeLine/7-1930-1999/hitler.html.

"How do genes tell the story of our ancient ancestor migration?" *Human Genome Project Human Migration.* January 12, 2012.http://www.ornl.gov/sci/techresources/Human_Genome/elsi/humanmigration.shtml.

Hunter, Darden. "Personality Disorder, Causes of Sociopathic Behavior." http://www.ehow.com/about_5125823_causes -sociopathic-behavior.html

Jekelius. Erwin Dr. *Yahoo Answers.* http://answers.yahoo.com/question/index?qid =20091123213024AAJwxQp.

Joachimsthaler, Anton. *Hitlers Liste: Ein Dokument Personlicher Beziehungen.* Herbig.

"Johann-Georg-Hiedler" *Factbites.* http://www.factbites.com/topics/Johann-Georg-Hiedler.

Joos, Dieter. "A Brief Description of a Southern German Village in the Past Centuries." *German Village* http://geisheimer.org/info/germ/village.htm.

Klein, John, and Adam Spears. *Devils and Demons and the Return of the Nephilim.* Fairfax: Xulon Press, 2005.

Langer, Walter C. *The Mind of Adolf Hitler; the Secret Wartime Report.* New York: Basic, 1972. Print.

Legacy of the Ancient Egyptian. http://legacyoftheancientegyptians.weebly.com/ancient-egyptian-legacy.html.

Machtan, Lothar 'The Hidden Hitler." http://www.angelfire.com/linux/thehiddenhitler/.

McQuick, Ms. O. Rene. "Antisocial-Personality-Disorder-Nature-or-Nurture?" *Docstoc.com.* http://www.docstoc.com/docs/976127/Antisocial-Personality-Disorder-Nature-or-Nurture

"Merriam-Webster." *Merriam-Webster*, n.d. Web. 18 Sept. 2012. <http://www.merriam-webster.com/>.

"Nazis gassed Hitler's relative." 'http://news.bbc.co.uk/2/hi/europe/4187823.stm

Nienhuis, James I. "Sons of Canaanite Posidon of Atlit were Ancestors of Berber and Tuareg Tribes of Northwest Africa Showing Atlantean Connection through Usage of Atl Etymology for Water." *Dancing from Genesis.* http://dancingfromgenesis.wordpress.com/2007/10/26/sons-of-canaanite-posidon-of-atlit-were-ancestors-of-berber-and-tuareg-tribes-of-northwest-africa-showing-atlantean-connection-through-usage-of-atl-etymology-for-water/.

Penchoen, Thomas G. "Berbers." *Encyclopedia.com*.http://www.encyclopedia.com/topic/Berbers.aspx.

"Psychopaths have brain structure abnormality." Examiner.com.

"Psychopathy An Important Forensic Concept for the 21st Century." *FBI.* N.p., n.d. Web. <http://www.fbi.gov/stats-services/publications/law-enforcement-bulletin/july-2012/focus-on-psychopathy.

"Psychopathy Traits in Children Becoming Alarmingly Familiar to More Parents." *ABC News Radio* Thu, 03 Nov 2011. http://www.sott.net/articles/show/237326-Psychopathy-Traits-in-Children-Becoming-Alarmingly-Familiar-to-More-Parents.

Ritenbaugh, Richard T. "Who were the Philistines?" http://www.cgg.org/index.cfm/fuseaction/Library.sr/CT/PW/k/1183/Who-Were-Philistines.htm#ixzz1gSjjfRrS.

Rosenbaum, Ron. *Explaining Hitler: The Search for the Origins of His Evil*. New York: Random House, 1998.

Sand, Jay. "Jews of Africa." http://www.mindspring.com/~jaypsand/morocco2.htm.

Schwarts, Jeffrey H. and Tattersall, Ian. "Hominids and Hybrids: The place of Neanderthals in Human Evolution." http://www.pnas.org/content/96/13/7117.long.

Seawright, Caroline. "Ancient Egyptian Sexuality." http://www.touregypt.net/featurestories/sexuality.htm.

"Sephardic Gen Resources." http://www.sephardicgen.com/seph_who.htm.

"The History of Israel – Sons of Noah." http://www.israel-a-history-of.com/sons-of-noah.html#<u>Ham - son of Noah</u>.

Thesaurus.com. http://thesaurus.com/browse/N.p.

Twin Study Finds Genetic Cause for Psychopathy. Future Pundit. http://www.sott.net/articles/show/147815-Twins-Study-Finds-Genetic-Cause-For-Psychopathy. June 23, 2013.

72 Interesting Facts about Adolf Hitler. N.p., n.d. Web. 06 Apr. 2013. <http://facts.randomhistory.com/hitler-facts.html>.

Vallely, Paul. "The Big Question: What's the history of Polygamy and how serious a problem is it in Africa?" *The Independent.* http://www.independent.co.uk/news/world/africa/the-big-question-whats-the-history-of-polygamy-and-how-serious-a-problem-is-it-in-africa-1858858.html.

Weiner, Rebecca. "Sephardim." http://www.jewishvirtuallibrary.org/jsource/Judaism/Sephardim.html

Wood, Larry. "Mystery Babylon the Great" http://www.biblenews1.com/babylon/babylon3.html.

Author Contact Information

Author V. Bryan
May be contacted through

Dominion and Glory Ministries

1046 Church Rd, W 106-224
Southaven, MS 38671

www.endtimenephilim.com